LIVING AND LEARNING
FROM THE HEALING WATERS
OF COURAGE

LIVING AND LEARNING FROM THE

HEALING WATERS OF COURAGE

BY HEATHER D. WRIGHT

COURTESY OF COLORFUL SPIRIT PUBLISHING

DEDICATION

This book is dedicated to God, my family, and friends who have all inspired me along the way. Thank you for all the special lessons you have taught me. I will always be eternally grateful.

COPYRIGHT INFORMATION

© 2014 by Heather D. Wright

ISBN 978-0-9859633-3-0

Published by Colorful Spirit Publishing

117 Winklers Meadow
Boone, NC 28607

www.colorfulspirit.com

Printed in the United States of America

CONTENTS

Introduction

Every now and then comes a time in our lives when we all need a touch of courage. Every single day we each long for something to give us joy and increase our strength. We all want to feel that there are lessons to be learned, and yet more than that, we hope we can heal from all the pain that has tried to break us down. There are days when it seems that we cannot make it through and wonder what we are here for and why God allows certain things to happen over which we have no control.

In this book, you will find lessons that will both give you courage and heal your broken heart. There are inspirational messages and poems meant to encourage you and help you discover all that God would want you to be. We all make mistakes in life, but God gives us the right path to embrace the healing waters of courage that will make us forever strong and able to overcome all the odds that try to make or break us.

As you read *Living and Learning from the Healing Waters of Courage*, it is my desire that you realize everything in life happens for a reason. Even when we do not always understand all of the reasons, we must trust that God is in control and will help us find the right solutions to the destined paths upon which we travel. I decided to share many of my life lessons with you in both a nonfiction and poetic way to illustrate the spiritual truths that have helped me find the courage to heal from my past and embrace happier, healthier times now and always. I hope the courageous chapters you are about to read encourage your hearts and souls in the most spiritual ways possible.

CHAPTER 1 - A GAMBLE WITH THE WINDS OF CHANGE

Sometimes We Must Take Risks to Change and Grow.

In life there are times events happen that do not make sense. There are moments when it seems we barely can find the strength to face a brand new day. There are some days life seems certain and all the signs point to good beginnings. Then there are nights when the fears of change consume us so much that it feels like we are drowning under the inability to take a chance in order to move forward. Life is all about taking risks because without the risks we take, we may never know that which we were meant to learn in the first place.

The following poem, "A Gamble with the Winds of Change", is about one person's search for greater meaning in his or her life. This poem is the struggle of someone so eager to change his life and feeling as if he or she has no place to turn until God sends a special friend in the form of an eagle who helps him find the courage to face his fears and embrace all the winds of change that come his way. When you feel all alone and as if nobody truly cares, this poem is one about taking a chance and knowing that no matter which way the wind blows, there will come a true friend who will love you and be right by your side no matter what.

———————————————————

A Gamble with the Winds of Change

I was sailing on a boat on
The big ocean we call life
When a wind so strong struck my sails
Filling my spirit with so much strife.

I held onto the sailboat
During a storm of uncertain times
In the midst of the cloudy skies I asked God
Why do I have to suffer so much and always ask why?

The answers did not come and after so much
Time had passed I made it back to shore.
I was greeted by a gentle breeze telling me to
Keep the faith so I will be blessed with so much more.

Filled with hope and wondering
What in the world I should expect
The winds of change blew me right into a
Valley that immediately scared me to death.

I was paralyzed by fear and begged God to send me
Some wind to lift me right out of despair
Yet I was trapped by the howling winds of sadness
From all the moments when it seemed nobody cared.

I reached for God to free me from this valley
Where life was way too hard
Then he sent a cool wind to pick me up and blow me
Right to a mountain that touched my broken heart.

I closed my eyes and could feel a gentle, warm breeze
Caress my much weary soul
As the calming wind lifted my spirits
I searched within for the spiritual strength to help me grow.

Feeling that maybe I could take some kind of gamble
To get my life going in the right direction
This time I hoped some wind could blow me
Far away from the grip of constant rejection.

I made a bet with nature and asked a golden eagle
If I could take a trip on his wings.
He picked me up and flew right against the unpredictable,
Shifting winds with such strength and ease.

I was now flying so high with a true friend
To keep me from falling from grace.
When the winds of time became challenging
He protected me always and kept me safe.

There were still storms that came but

I was determined not to let anything make me fall.
The eagle was my kindred spirit helping me endure tough
winds
So nothing could break me down at all.

During days when the sun was shining
And there was hardly a breeze in sight
I could feel a cool air coming from the eagle's wings
Reassuring me everything would be all right.

Through all the changing seasons and the
Winds of time that brought surprises my way
I just kept flying high with the eagle who was
There to help me endure my not so good days.

When the winds of change did not always offer
The certain path I wanted to pursue
I knew God had sent me a special kind of
Loving friend who remained forever true.

I have taken gambles all my life with the
Winds of change not knowing which way to turn.
As I look back on my past choices I realized during
The strongest winds there was so much to learn.

Every now and then when I take a gamble on
The winds of change hoping for the best
I know I have a true love in the eagle who calms
All the wind to help me survive life's greatest tests.

CHAPTER 2 - A SPIRITUAL STRUGGLE BETWEEN A DARK AND LIGHT PATH

Even If We Get Thrown Off Track, God Helps Us Get Back on Our Feet Again.

If there is one word that I have come to know well, it would be struggle. I have struggled most of my life to the point that I would not know what life was like without such difficulty. It seems there have been times I did not think I was going to survive, but somehow God allowed me to get back on track. The one thing I realized early on in my life is that sometimes God takes us off the path upon which we find ourselves. Sometimes He allows us to go through tough times to teach us the greatest lessons that we are meant to learn.

The following poem, "A Spiritual Struggle Between a

Dark and a Light Path", addresses one soul's search to find balance in his life. It seems his life is going all well, but he still has to face the fact that with the good the bad is destined to happen too. No matter how much we hope to escape hard times, the truth is that we are all destined to experience good and bad moments in life. We just have to keep the faith that everything will work out for the best when we remain courageous and strong.

——————————————————

A Spiritual Struggle Between A Dark and Light Path

I was walking along a path
That so many people often travel
And for some reason I thought just like them
I could make it on my own without coming unraveled.

Before I knew what had hit me
I was thrust into a dark tunnel full of despair.
And I kept hearing loud voices shout
We want your soul to know that nobody does care.

I was crying from the inside out not sure
How to escape the lonely abyss that held me back.
All I knew was I needed to figure out
How much longer I would feel lost before I got back on track.

Days and nights passed and I just prayed

God would somehow set me free.
Yet deep within my broken spirit
I was drowning under self-imposed misery.

After prayers of desperation to see the light
After walking through a world where darkness reigned,
I was thrust onto a new path of rosy red flowers
With the sun shining down after a long, hard rain.

On this path I was so happy now because
There were birds and butterflies dancing around my feet.
I felt God sent them to be my new friends
Full of hope who had the secret to overcoming defeat.

We played together in the field of great dreams
With a gentle breeze and the sun shining all around.
I could close my eyes and feel the breath of Heaven
Nourish my soul with the most peaceful sound.

Everywhere I turned I knew that I was
In a place of utter and complete peace.
I could see the leaves on trees that had budded freely
To the sounds of spring's harmonious release.

After spending many wonderful days
Enjoying the brightness of light and courage,
I noticed the world around me grew dark again
Leaving me confused and once again discouraged.

Bewildered by the sudden change in my good fortune
I was angry and asked God why now.

He just whispered I'm still with you but
You got to stumble sometimes to grow stronger somehow.

Upset and eager to escape this dark world
Where I once was a prisoner of pain.
I could still hear God whisper I'm still your friend
And will help you endure this present shame.

I wanted to give up because it seemed
The world I left was just an illusion I could not find again.
Yet in the midst of all my questions I could feel
God whisper sometimes you have to lose to win.

As the days of continual darkness and constant confusion
Continued to break me apart,
I started getting on my hands and knees
Asking God to help free my most troubled heart.

With tears of the deepest sadness
I could feel God encouraging me to never give up.
He said you have to have faith
And the time will come when you will have much better
luck.

After many sleepless nights I found myself
Waking up to the sun shining again on my face.
When the nights of darkness ended
I could feel a new strength built on a much greater faith.

In this new world I was seeing the creation of
God's glory in a different way than before.

I could feel the positive energies of nature
Loving me even deeper and forevermore.

I was curious and wondering why things
Seemed different in this world where I once felt so safe.
I now felt more energy to keep going so that
When the darkness came I was able now to get away.

I could feel more faith, hope, and love
Refreshing my spirit when I learned to let God take control.
Now my life was no longer an unfortunate struggle
But a spiritual haven always protecting my soul.

CHAPTER 3 -
CAUGHT BETWEEN
POSITIVE AND
NEGATIVE ENERGY

We Must Keep the Faith During the Highs and Lows of Life.

Life is never easy for any of us to face. There are times when it seems everything is working out just the way we hope where so many things are falling into place. Then there are times it seems everything is falling apart around us and there is nothing we can do to keep such hardships from destroying us from the inside out.

I am a lover of positive energy, and as hard has it is, I strive to be optimistic. On the other hand, the negative forces of this life can easily weigh me down so I have to be careful. I can feel on top of the world one day and then all it takes the next day is one wrong word or one inappropriate action to send me spiraling down into the depths of sadness. My entire life has been a struggle to stay on the positive side of life, but I have also come to realize that I have to face that there will be dark times too. When these dark times come, I know that I have to make sure I do not lose sight of the joy within me.

The following poem, "Caught Between Positive and Negative Energy", addresses the constant battle these two forces fight within one's soul and the different ways good and bad energy affect all of us.

_____

Caught Between Positive and Negative Energy

Sometimes I feel like I am
On top of the world.
Life seems to be bringing me the fruits
Of the spirit without any turmoil.

Sometimes I feel like I can make anything
Happen with a smile and a gamble with chance.
Nothing can bring me down because I am met
With good fortune and the right circumstance.

Sometimes I feel like nothing is ever
Working out the way I hope.
There are days it is all I can do to
Survive and find the strength to cope.

Sometimes all I want to do is run away
From all my setbacks.

Yet I feel bound by an internal struggle of defeat
That keeps me feeling off track.

Sometimes I think that God has given me
So many great things for which I am thankful.
I can say many prayers of hope because with faith
There is no need to feel dreadful.

Sometimes I feel that my life is working
Out just the way I had planned.
There are times all things fall in place when
The rest of the world does not understand.

Sometimes I feel like I am
Suffocating from the inside out.
It is like a negative energy attacks my good soul
And keeps it drowning in a world of doubt.

Sometimes I feel like the harder I try,
The harder I fail.
No matter how much I try to make things right
The depressing times seem to prevail.

Sometimes I feel like I can conquer any of my
Worst fears through good times and bad.
I can trust God above to lead me on the
Right path without always feeling so sad.

Sometimes I can find a rainbow
On the cloudiest day before me.

It is as if my spirit can
Overcome the greatest misery.

Sometimes I feel like I am so depressed
I just want to quit my life.
It is like the misfortunes gather around my soul
And keep me submerged in a world of strife.

Sometimes I feel like the pain
From my past never seems to end.
And then again I suffer the betrayal
Of a once trusted friend.

Sometimes I think that all my troubles
Will be a thing of the past.
The more I keep the faith, the more I see
The hard times will not last.

Sometimes I feel that nothing can keep
Me feeling down and upset.
I trust that God will give me the right intuition
To have faith and not live in a mindset of regret.

Sometimes I feel my broken spirit will
Always remain completely torn apart.
It is as if I remain isolated in shame wounded
By the false charms of a misguided heart.

Sometimes I just do not know
How much more I can take.

At times I feel my life is worthless
And just one great big mistake.

Sometimes I really wonder if I will overcome
The energies that want to own my soul.
I just pray to God that He will somehow
Send enough love so the light never lets me go.

CHAPTER 4 - EVERYTHING HAPPENS FOR A REASON

There is a Purpose for Everything We Experience.

Life is full of events that I feel shape who we are meant to become. From the time we are children and become adults, we are meant to go through so many different life experiences. The challenges in life we face I feel can either make us or break us depending on how we choose to respond. I have never been a firm believer in coincidences. In fact, I feel that all the mistakes we make and all the decisions we choose influence who we are to become.

The following poem, "Everything Happens for a Reason", discusses the journey of a soul at sea facing many challenges to overcome as he battles raging storms and harsh winds. Through his journey over the uncertain

waters of life, he comes to realize that everything does
really happen for a reason.

Everything Happens for a Reason

I was sailing on an ocean in the
Vast waters we call life,
Thinking I might have a story to tell about
The ups and downs of living and my perpetual whys.

Time and time again I felt I was meant
To sail an unconventional path at sea.
There were so many times I felt lost to
Misguided choices and confusing mysteries.

During some of my sails at sea life
Was as great as I had ever dreamed.
On the surface things were going well
And my journey was just as I felt I wanted it to be.

I could sail to the top of the highest wave
And feel I had conquered all my fears.
When life was good, I knew things flowed smoothly
So I could avoid drowning under unwanted tears.

Thinking I was meant to sail a peaceful journey at sea
Without any trouble to come my way,
Before I realized what was happening it was as if
An uncertain darkness took my sunshine away.

The winds of change blew so hard and the sky grew
So dark and dreary I did not know what to do,
Yet somewhere I heard a still small voice above me say,
"Trust me to inspire you to make it through".

The sails on my boat were beaten so hard as if
I no longer had control over my desired direction.
My once confident demeanor changed into
A frightened soul longing for protection.

The waves were crashing so hard against my sailboat
That I barely felt I could survive.
Somehow I knew this must be happening
To help me not give up and always try.

Frustrated beyond measure and thinking God
Had somehow interfered with my chosen fate,
I could hear Him whisper, "I am trying to make your
Soul stronger so sometimes you have to wait".

Not really sure if I wanted to hear the words
That I was meant to suffer before I would be set free,
The winds of uncertainty and waves of fear kept crashing
Around my boat of refuge so profusely.

After many long days and nights with harsh weather
From the ocean trying to break me down,
I wished I'd learned from my mistakes instead of living
To the tune of my own preferred sound.

Thinking there was a reason I was meant to go through

This time of change and worrisome cries.
Somewhere deep within my heart I needed to heal
Past wounds from my heart for good this time.

Through the struggles I encountered along
What I thought would be smooth sailing.
God helped me realize I had succeeded in being stronger
Now though it felt my spirit was failing.

After all the unpredictable winds and waves of change
Made me feel I could hardly cope,
When I thanked God for saving me,
I knew I was a new person now with a heart full of hope.

CHAPTER 5 - FALLING BACK, MOVING FORWARD

Sometimes We Have to Take a Step Back and Put Ourselves in Someone Else's Shoes in Order to Gain a New Perspective and Move Forward.

I have discovered that we often need to really take a step back at times and try to see life through the eyes and experiences of other people. When it comes to life experience, I really feel we learn best when we can focus on life from different viewpoints. I am very empathetic to the needs of others, and I feel when we really try to understand what someone else has been through it helps us have more insight and wisdom as to why people do what they do.

Playing different roles in life teaches us so much. It could be that through the different hats we wear and the various games we play, that we discover something new about ourselves. In the same fashion, being able to revisit the past or escaping into a dream has a way of teaching us certain lessons. By remembering the past or living out new choices through dreams and fantasies, we can reconnect with a part of ourselves when we felt strong and happy or connect to a part of ourselves we never knew existed through the power of our dreams.

The following poem, "Falling Back, Moving Forward", addresses one soul's imagination of a fantasy world where he dreams of living in different time periods. Through his fantasy of these various journeys through time, he comes to understand more about himself by living his life through the experiences of others.

───────────────────────────────

Falling Back and Moving Forward

I was falling back in time
Hoping to find my way.
I felt destined to learn from souls from lifetimes past
Who knew me well when I fell from grace.

I prayed that my travels back in time would
Help me solve the mysterious cries of my heart.
It was as if I was meant to learn spiritual truths
To keep me strong so I would not fall apart.

In one lifetime I was a lost soul who
Never seemed to catch a break,
Yet I met one soul who taught me bad luck
Makes you value good fortune when it comes to stay.

In one lifetime I was a poor beggar
Who seemed to struggle to make ends meet,
But I met a soul who stopped everyday to make sure
I was ok and had good food to eat.

In one lifetime I had so much money
I did not know where to spend it all,
And then a soul came along and said make sure
You share the wealth so your pride does not let you fall.

In one lifetime I was a teacher thinking I could
Change the world with one lesson of good instruction,
Yet I met a soul who said you can't know it all
Unless you have learned the art of surviving destruction.

In one lifetime I was not always the
Easiest person for anyone to be around,
And when I tried to remain negative
One soul came by to turn my frown upside down.

In one lifetime I was so happy that everyone
Wanted to know my secret to success.
Then one unlucky soul said I need you to believe in me
So I can handle life's hard tests.

In one lifetime I was so confused that
I did not know where to turn.
Then one soul stood beside me as the tears wet my feet
With such devotion and heartfelt concern.

In one lifetime I was always trying to put my needs

Above those around me because I did not care,
Yet as soon as I turned my back some soul reminded me
Those who loved me would always be there.

In one lifetime I was just a child with such
An innocent look of trust nobody could escape.
I met a like-minded soul with a gentle heart like mine
That could share in my most hopeful ways.

In one lifetime I was all alone with nobody
That I could feel I could trust,
And then one soul came along to say I will be
The friend you need and will never let you give up.

In one lifetime I was so in love that I felt
There were no limits on the passing of time,
Then the soul who loved me unconditionally said
We will always speak the same rhythm and rhyme.

In this lifetime I was all the things I never wanted to be
And yet all the things God desired,
Yet on the inside all my past lives were echoing the lessons
My travels had taught me that would never expire.

When I dream of the future I am not sure what lifetime
I will be living as the past and present collide,
All I know is all the souls who crossed my path
Gave my inner spirit courage to stay strong and never die.

CHAPTER 6 -
FINDING COURAGE
DURING THE STORM

When Storms Come Into Our Lives, We Can Conquer Them.

Storms are inevitable in our lives. It is not possible to live life without facing hard times. No matter how much we want the good times to never end, we have to realize that it is through storms that God makes us stronger. I have been through so many storms in my own life from broken relationships to financial despair that I barely thought I would have the strength to survive. I can remember questioning why I had to go through so many tough moments, and then looking back I realized I was meant to go through the storm so I could find the courage to know with God's help I could face anything that came my way.

The following poem, "Finding Courage During the Storm", is a reflection of all the fears and uncertainties that often try to make us or break us. I actually was inspired to write this poem based on a true thunder storm I was driving through one night. In the midst of my drive, I remember feeling so scared and was praying that God would help me find my way back home. Even though the storm was rough, God did give me the courage to stay strong which inevitably helped me find my way back to where I knew I could feel safe and secure. After having this experience, I related it to true storms we all face in different areas of our lives and realized that God will give us courage to come out stronger on the other side if we just believe we will survive.

Finding Courage During the Storm

I was driving along a highway
On a cold, rainy night.
For a brief time it felt my world
Was feeling stable and all right.

In the blink of an eye everything
Around me seemed to change.
What was once calm and peaceful within me
Was met by a relentless, hard rain.

The rain was pouring down so hard on
My car window that I could barely see.
It was as if I was reminded of the times
I felt discouraged and could barely find the strength to
breathe.

I knew I needed to drive carefully for fear
I could have a bad wreck,
Yet the puddles of water standing in the road
Kept me sliding everywhere as if I was faced with regrets.

I thought maybe I should just pull over and let
All the cars driving so fast just past me by.
Then I was reminded of the times I let others push me
around
Leaving me frustrated and asking why.

Determined to keep going no matter how much
The stormy weather tried to hold me back.
As much as I wanted to stop the car and let the storm pass,
I knew I had to stay on track.

Throughout the entire time on my journey
The rain just kept falling so hard,
And the roar of thunder became so loud
It drowned out the fearful beating of my desperate heart.

Praying I would somehow make it home
Far away from this nightmare of a drive,
The lightening strikes reminded me of the times
I was struck down by such pain I could hardly survive.

Wondering if the storm would ever stop and give me
A much needed break from my despair,
The scary side of nature brought back memories
Of the wounds in my soul from those who never cared.

After a time of driving through a storm
That I thought would never end,
I asked God to help me find the courage to trust
His guidance because I needed a most loyal friend.

Afraid I was completely on my own with
No friend to help me along the way,
I looked up and saw a bright full moon
Enlightening my journey with such grace.

Even though the storm seemed like
It was going to last forever,
I just focused on the light from the moon shining down
As if God had given me a much needed treasure.

When the stormy clouds tried to cover the moon
That had become my much needed guide,
I just looked within and found the courage to trust
This was nature's way of keeping me safe and alive.

With new courage in my spirit and a desire
To make it home no matter what,
I knew God had sent a full moon in the midst of storm
To help me keep the faith and never let my hope stop.

CHAPTER 7 - LIVING AND LEARNING

Life is All About Living and Learning from Our Mistakes.

The following poem, "Living and Learning", is the central theme of this entire book which makes this particular poem the cornerstone upon which this book is written. We all have a destiny, and I truly believe that every choice we make and every mistake we encounter is meant to help us along life's way.

The more we struggle, the more we learn that so many things are truly out of our control so we must let go and let God take over when we are unable to handle life on our own. We live and learn, and then we live and learn some more. It is so true that not only does life go on, but the lessons we come to appreciate shape our hearts and strengthen our spirits so we can keep living and learning to our full potential.

———————————————

Living and Learning

I was writing a book about all
The lessons I had learned.
Somewhere along the way I was reminded
Of the times I had been hurt.

When I reflected back on the past
To a time when life was hard,
Somehow I knew God had given me
The strength to make it this far.

I prayed often and asked God
To help give me some kind of sign.
He just remained silent and whispered
You have to learn from your mistakes this time.

Frustrated and confused because of
All the setbacks I had faced,
The determination within me kept growing
To remain strong and not run away.

As I looked deep within to figure out
What choices I should pursue,
Even with a broken heart at times,
I knew I was meant to learn a lesson or two.

No matter which way I looked and
No matter what path I chose to travel,
I had to face the fact that sometimes
Life may come unraveled.

Encouraged to keep fighting when

Everything around me seemed to fall apart,
I just kept the faith that one day God would
Help heal my forever wounded heart.

At times when life was crazy and all
The voices of despair tried to break me down,
I just had to believe that one day the chaos
Would give way to a more peaceful sound.

After being torn so much from
Left to right and side to side,
All I knew was I needed to trust
There are times I don't need to ask why.

During my journeys when sailing against the storm
Seemed the right thing to do,
I could still hear God's voice whisper
Trust your instincts and life will be good to you.

After every page I turned in
My own book called life,
The chapters that were the hardest to read
Were the ones marked with tremendous strife.

Even when I found myself crying
Because the words were so hard to read,
I just prayed hard and ask God to give
My broken spirit fresh, serene air to breathe.

I often am reminded of the lessons I have learned
Throughout the time I have been alive.

As much as I embrace the good memories
I often am haunted by the moments I wanted to die.

As I write a few more chapters in the story
Of one's soul journey to be loved and protected forever,
My heart finds peace in an agape kind of love
That lives within a kindred spirit God gave me to treasure.

CHAPTER 8 - MY LUCKY WALK IN THE PARK OF NEW BEGINNINGS

Sometimes We Must Take a Chance on a New Beginning.

Let's face it. Life is hard for all of us and sometimes all we need is a brand new start in life. There have been many times I felt that things in my life were not working out as I had hoped. Many times it felt like I was just running into brick walls when what I really wanted was a chance to just start over and correct all the mistakes I have made throughout my life.

The problem is so many of us are afraid of change and to take the risks that we know will make us feel that everything is falling into place for us exactly the way we so desire. The following poem, "A Lucky Walk in the Park of New Beginnings", is all about taking chances and not being afraid to be happier.

A Lucky Walk in the Park Of New Beginnings

I was walking down a brand new nature path
That seemed truly inviting.
There was something about the lure of an adventure
That appeared so exciting.

The more I walked this path
The more I knew it was time for me to break free.
I was sick and tired of everyone else
Trying to explain how my life should be.

I took a few steps and saw a tree
With apples so fresh that caught my eye.
So I took a bite feeling something good
Was about to happen in my life.

Full of joy and hopeful for what
My next stop would eventually bring.
I saw a red cardinal singing
Sweet lullabies just meant for me.

As I journeyed a little further
I ran across a butterfly so sweet and true.
When I leaned a little closer to it I could feel it whisper
I will always believe in you.

I then came across a row of yellow roses
Whose beauty charmed my soul.

Their sweet fragrance made me feel
What love feels like in a world gone cold.

I continued walking and saw two morning doves
Sitting together on the ground.
The doves cried out keep the faith
That true friends won't let you down.

With a renewed spirit I felt that I enjoyed
All God wanted me to see and feel.
Then a red-winged black bird flew beside me
To protect me with a love that's real.

I could hardly believe all the new discoveries
That crossed my destined path.
When I looked to the sky I felt
There were no clouds of fear holding me back.

I came to a park bench where I decided
To take a short break on my new walk.
Then a little squirrel came by sensing
I needed a friend too with whom I can talk.

When I reached the end of my path
I thought of all God had sent my way.
Everything I met on my new path was God's cry
To be strong and keep the faith.

My soul was flooded with past memories
And the discoveries I was led to make.

I learned true happiness lies within
And false promises do fade away.

CHAPTER 9 -
ROADBLOCKS AND
DETOURS THAT LED
TO A BETTER LIFE

Sometimes Hitting a Brick Wall Leads to a New Direction.

Life is a constant series of roadblocks. One minute it seems everything is going great and the pieces of the puzzle are falling into place. Then the next minute something difficult we never expected to face almost knocks us down to the point it seems like we are not going to survive.

I have discovered that with all the roadblocks we face, there are also detours God provides to give us a chance to find the right path at the moment we need it most. The more we endure setbacks, the stronger we become and the easier it becomes for us to take a detour that will finally lead us to much greater paths of happiness.

In the following poem, "Roadblocks and Detours that Led to a Better Life", there are many roadblocks revealed yet there is equal determination to find a detour that leads away from constant pain into a place where life is more peaceful and joyful.

––––––––––––––––––––––

Roadblocks and Detours that Led to a Better Life

I ran into a crazy roadblock
I never expected to face.
Somehow I knew I need to remain strong
So I would not fall from grace.

I found a nice detour
That took me on a brand new path.
Others thought I should stay right where I was
But I wanted to move on without looking back.

I pushed full steam ahead and yet
Another roadblock tried to keep me from growing,
Yet within my weary spirit I felt I was destined for change
And held on to this spiritual knowing.

I took another detour where my dreams
Finally could come true.
Then I caught a glimpse of a hopeful sunset
Asking me to keep the faith and quit feeling so blue.

I got back on my feet again thinking
All was well until another roadblock knocked me down.

This time I took a moment to assess my situation
Before my worries sent me running out of town.

I found another detour with a magical entrance
To a world where there was peace.
The moment I embraced this energy
I could feel my stress give way like a much needed release.

I had a fresh vision of a life I needed
Before a new roadblock blew my way.
Then I questioned when the negative energy
Would quit ruining my more joyful days.

I knew despite this mishap another charming detour
Awaited to keep me safe from deceit.
The lovely path upon which I now walked
Was full of flowers surviving cold winters without defeat.

I thought this time I could finally be happy
Until another roadblock kept me from walking.
The more I tried to drown out the unhealthy energies
The louder they just kept talking.

After all these roadblocks I asked God
To help me find a spiritual detour away from all my worry.
He sent a rainbow with a box of spiritual treasures
Promising to bless my life with a brand new story.

It's amazing how I had to endure
A mix of roadblocks and detours to find the path for my life.

The spiritual strength I gained along the way
Reassures me everything will be all right.

CHAPTER 10 - SPIRITUAL TRANSFORMATION IN THE MIDST OF TRIBULATION

When We Learn to Let Go and Let God, Miracles Can Occur.

There have been so many times in my life that I have wanted to give up. Ever since I was a little girl, I never really felt like I fit in to the mainstream world. In fact, trying to be what everyone else wanted me to be has created tremendous inner turmoil for me my entire life.

I used to think that in order to really be happy, I had to make everyone else happy in the process. However, what I discovered is that I was the one who suffered the most and until I found the right path of spiritual fulfillment that would be the only time real joy would erupt in my life.

The following poem, "Spiritual Transformation in the

Midst of Tribulation", was written after what I call one of my many dark nights of the soul. I have to admit that I fall victim to many negative energy attacks on my spirit, yet with God's ultimate mercy and healing, He always has given me the inner strength to work through my despair so that I begin a brand new path feeling able to overcome any adversity.

Spiritual Transformation in the Midst of Tribulation

Something was telling me
There was about to come a change,
Yet my disappointed spirit was afraid
I would be let down again drowning in shame.

In the midst of the chaos of a life
I wish I had not ever produced,
I found myself very tired and begging
For a way to have my stress finally reduced.

Days and nights passed and I wondered
When would I ever catch a break.
Trusting in the world to lead me
In the best direction was my largest mistake.

I took some walks outside with
So many tears in my eyes I could barely see.
I was not sure if I should keep fighting
Or give in to the world's illusion of a life filled with misery.

On a cloudy day in the middle of
What appeared to be spring
I was greeted by a red-winged black bird
That acted as if he had really missed me.

Then I was reminded of the times I had been to this place
Where my spiritual essence was on fire,
Yet I had let the craziness of life
Destroy my inner joy that had grown weary and tired.

As I looked into the eyes of the red-winged black bird
He told me my soul would grow strong again.
Like so many times in the past he always knew
When I needed the help of a very good friend.

With a new smile on my face I decided to keep
Walking this path that seemed different this time.
When I looked to the sky I could hear God
Play a sweet melody of peace with a harmonious rhyme.

I was curious to see what else I had missed
While being trapped in a world of despair.
When I looked ahead I saw a familiar yellow butterfly
Flap its wings to tell me she still cared.

Amazed and in awe of this new path
That seemed full of reminders of what I had loved and lost
Letting the negative energy of other people and things
Had crushed my spirit at an unhealthy cost.

It is funny now as I look back and

See all the times I let life bring me down.
With God on my side I discovered a brand new faith
To help me turn my misguided life back around.

CHAPTER 11 - THE BEAUTIFUL BUTTERFLY THAT ESCAPED ITS DARK COCOON

God Does Not Intend for Us to Be Trapped Within a World of Misery As He Desires to Set Our Imprisoned Spirits Free.

I think the worse feeling in the world is to feel like you are suffocating under a blanket of despair. There are times we all long for a life that is free from constant pain and stress. In a world drowning in negativity, it is often very hard to know how to overcome challenges and problems.

The following poem, "The Beautiful Butterfly that Escaped Its Dark Cocoon" is a special story about a butterfly who realizes the cocoon that has become his home is no longer a safe place to dwell. After many long days and nights of constant struggles, the butterfly finally finds the strength to break free from its world of darkness. Along his new journey, he meets and befriends a special daisy that changes his life forever. If you feel as if there is no way to escape a life that is no longer working for you, just have faith that you can find your way onto a path of freedom marked with truth and real beauty.

The Beautiful Butterfly that Escaped its Dark Cocoon

Once upon a time there was a cocoon
With a caterpillar who wanted to break free.
He kept crying within his shell
How long will it take before I can escape such misery.

No matter where he turned it seemed
That his cocoon was so hard to break.
The harder he tried to stay strong he still felt
His life was a series of badly made mistakes.

Days and nights went by and the
Caterpillar struggled to and fro.
Somehow he managed to feel lost
In a world of broken promises where he longed to let go.

After so many evenings of nightmares
Wondering when he would finally see the light,
The caterpillar just prayed and asked God to protect his

soul
So at some point he would feel all right.

Inside of his dark world he could hear
His own heart crying for a new chance.
On the outside world he wished to be
Part of those caught in a world of great circumstance.

The scared caterpillar wondered so much
When the time his fate would change.
In the midst of his fears he kept the faith
That one day he would emerge from his wall of shame.

One spring day when the sun was shining brightly
And the sky was crystal blue,
The caterpillar noticed a small hole on its cocoon
Where a bright light shined through and through.

Excited that maybe this was a chance to escape
Into a place where life was much better,
The caterpillar noticed it had lovely golden wings
So it could fly to new places no matter the weather.

With its bright orange wings and
Colorful flowers meant to color its fresh path,
The orange butterfly now could fly high above
All its hardships from the past without looking back.

From one flower to the next the butterfly
Flew to each one to gain nourishment for its heart.

He knew these flowers were his heavenly sent friends
That would never let him fall apart.

During his new journey in the middle of spring,
He grew to love a special daisy flower
With such beauty that he learned
What true love really means.

Even during the rainy days when it
Just wanted a place to feel safe, the orange butterfly
Knew the daisy would be his true friend
Who would love him til his dying day.

Every now and then no matter where
The orange butterfly may land,
Through all of nature's finest that now greets his path
He knows the admirable daisy always understands.

CHAPTER 12 - THE COLORFUL BALLOONS WITH SECRET LESSONS TO SHARE

Through the Innocence of Children and Their Love for Life, We Can Trust God Brings Us Important Truths Through Simple Pleasures.

I honestly have to say that I had a wonderful childhood. God truly blessed me with loving parents and a supportive home where I learned at an early age not to take for granted the simple pleasures of life. In fact, I was always fascinated with balloons and can remember watching in awe as a child as many colored balloons went soaring through the air. It made me happy, and it also made me curious if one day I would understand why God created so many balloons in so many colors.

The following poem, "The Colorful Balloons With Secret Lessons to Share", is based on a true experience I had at a children's birthday party I attended. After standing in a park for awhile, I noticed so many different children holding on to their balloons and when they let go of them, I once again, found myself in awe of their freedom to fly high. What interested me most is that I felt each balloon had a secret to share, and with great spiritual insight, I decided to write the following poem based on the wisdom I feel God imparted to me about these colorful balloons in the park that day.

The Colorful Balloons With Secret Lessons to Share

I was lost in a crowd of searching souls
On a hot summer day
When suddenly my eyes were drawn to
Colorful balloons all around me in different ways.

I watched a blue balloon drift
Out of the hands of a small child.
Even though he wanted to hold on to it,
He learned you have to let go once in awhile.

I looked around and saw one child
Holding onto her red balloon so much,
Yet she was not meant to get what she wanted
And had to learn to quit pushing her luck.

I moved a little closer to another boy who struggled
To catch his green balloon with his bare hands.
It seemed the higher he jumped to keep it from flying
He realized sometimes it's ok to not understand.

As I continued looking around I saw a young girl
Walking hand in hand with a yellow balloon.
She somehow could feel it was telling her
To not let go of her joy in life too soon.

When I saw another little boy who was crying
Because his orange balloon was already in the sky,
He learned that sometimes when life does not make sense
It is honestly ok to question why.

I watched another little girl who was screaming
For someone to bring her purple balloon back.
Somewhere in her confusion she learned to accept
That sometimes things happen to throw us off track.

I continued my observations only to find
A young boy willing to let his brown balloon go.
It was as if he had come to realize there are times
We grow stronger when we go with the flow.

As I continued looking around I saw a young girl
Refusing to let her pink balloon escape.
Yet in her struggle to do things her way,
She learned sometimes we have to cooperate anyway.

I eventually saw all these balloons drift

Closer to Heaven with their secrets to share.
I could feel God whisper it took a few colored balloons
To show you how much I do care.

With tears of joy in my eyes and a smile on my face
That had not been there for so long,
I thanked God for helping me learn
To keep the faith and remain forever strong.

CHAPTER 13 - THE CREATIVE CAT IN A WORLD OFF TRACK

The Lesson to Learn is that Animals Can Be a Source of Comfort and Inspiration to Us During the Ups and Downs of Our Lives.

I have always loved animals. In fact, I would have to say that my most favorite pet of all are cats. Ever since I was a little girl, I fell in love with every kitten and cat that decided to call my parent's house home. Even when mom told me that it was time for me to give up some kittens because we could not keep them all, I had a hard time parting ways with any of them. With every cat I have ever owned, I have felt a special bond. In fact, the cats I have loved and lost along the way have each taught me special lessons.

The following poem, "The Creative Cat in a World Off Track", is all about the special ways in which the energy of a precious cat that once lived is able to help his previous owner. Just as the owner felt his special cat friend by his side through every season of life, he continued to feel his cat's energy when he needed hope in the midst of crisis and courage to endure the storms of life. In fact, the creative energies of the owner's former cat serve as his spirit guide encouraging him to embrace a path of justice and truth knowing one day he will overcome all the odds against him.

The Creative Cat in a World Off Track

Once upon a time in a world
I never could quite understand,
I felt the spirit of a cat I had loved and lost
Whose energy was more powerful than the richest land.

There were people around me
Demanding so much from left to right.
I just wanted to ask them to leave me be
So I could finally sleep peacefully at night.

Some days it was all I could do to break through
The chains of doubt trying to break me down,
Yet in my lowest moment I could feel
The spirit of my dear cat who was determined to stick around.

I felt the whole world around me was feeling
Apathetic and eager for me to feel broken,

But in my heart the cat I lost left a mark
On my soul more precious than any monetary token.

Somehow I knew my spirit was drowning
Under a sea of great frustration.
In the midst of my worries I felt my cat
Was calming my waves of fear and hopeless desperation.

I wanted to find that spark in my soul
Where my creative energies could really flow.
When I looked within my insecure spirit
I knew still had a friend right beside me that loved me so.

Trying to find a way to bring back that part of myself
That the world had tried to crush.
I knew the cat whose spirit surrounded me
Was the driving force of strength to give me better luck.

During the moments I knew I needed something
To help me take the world by surprise.
I just thought of my precious cat
And felt her spirit of hope help me work through many lies.

It felt like the rest of the world was laughing
Because of the negative energy that would never escape.
Then the image of a cat who never gave up
Encouraged me to keep hanging in there for a better day.

After so many long days and nights of feeling
Trapped in a prison I so wanted to end.

I felt everyday now was a new journey
Where the cat I loved so much stayed as a trusted friend.

Even when the rest of the world
Tries to make me feel bad or as if I will never survive,
I just feel the sweet protective energies of the cat
Who watches out for me until it is my time to die.

It is funny how losing my dear friend
Was like losing a part of my soul,
Yet the creativity of her loving spirit
Has been the renewal of energy my spirit needed to grow.

The world may continue to bring me false promises
And people who really don't care,
But my cat's presence helps me feel inspired
By a kindred spirit I hope will always be there.

Creativity is the fuel that drives my heart
To beat with great faith all will be ok.
The sincere energies of my cat that died
Keeps me close to the kindred soul I love in many ways.

It really is amazing how it takes something you love
To die to feel a new life has begun.
I know the enduring love of a creative cat
In a world gone off track is the prize my soul has won.

CHAPTER 14 - THE CURIOUS COIN OF CHOICES AND CHANCES

We Have to Be Willing To Take Chances in Life and Have Faith That the Choices We Make Will Lead Us on The Right Path for Our Lives.

If there is one thing I came to realize early on in my life, it is that life is full of chances and choices. There was a time in my life where I was very afraid of taking chances because I always felt I would fail. I often did not trust my instincts and would go against my better judgment because I truly lacked confidence in myself. In fact, I thought risk taking was by nature a very dangerous feat when in all actuality I just let fear stop me every time.

The following poem, "The Curious Coin of Choices and Chances", is all about taking a chance on a new path in life. There are some people I feel who really like to flip a coin hoping that no matter where it falls that somehow they will find the answers to their destiny. I actually feel God can lead us to the right decision even through a simple coin toss. If you feel led one way when you toss the coin and it lands on heads, then maybe just maybe that is the path where you are meant to travel. If you toss the coin and it lands on tails and feel led to go that route, then as I have learned it is always best to trust your instincts and choose to take a chance on a new beginning.

The Curious Coin of Choices and Chances

I flipped a coin and wondered
Why it fell on the side of choice.
Maybe God truly heard my cry for help
Coming from a very frustrated voice.

When I flipped the coin again
And it fell on the side of chance,
I realized I needed to quit trying so hard
And trust some lessons come from bad circumstance.

I decided to flip the coin once more to see
How many times it would land on choice and change.
Somehow I could feel a spiritual presence whisper
I will protect you from shame.

I was not quite so sure I wanted to make a choice
And thought maybe I should flip my coin one more time.

I knew somehow I had to figure out how to quit
Letting others try to manipulate my restless mind.

I thought to myself that often flipping the coin
Could bring me back to the side of chance and dreams,
Yet an angel inside cried out just protect yourself
And know life is not always what it seems.

I was still not quite happy with the coin falling
On a chance where maybe the outcome seemed unfair,
But when I flipped my coin again I realized
There will always be some people that don't truly care.

Curious to find the hidden truths to the maze
Of lost hope that I felt this coin might give,
I just flipped it another time and it landed
On a choice I made to not look back and learn to forgive.

In flipping my coin and trying to understand
Where the chips may fall,
The next time I let it land on the side of chance
I knew giving up should not be in my vocabulary at all.

I was still determined to flip this curious coin
A few more times to get the answers I needed.
No matter where the coin landed this time,
I kept the faith knowing God would not let me be defeated.

I flipped this curious coin so much that
I found it kept falling on choice and sometimes chance.

When I tried to make sense of it all I knew
I had to make the best of life and use good common sense.

I was not sure if I could ever find the best
Clear cut solution to the problems that tried to tear me
apart,
Yet when I lay awake at night no matter where
The curious coin fell God healed my weary heart.

Everyday I pray God gives me the most trusted coin
That will fall and push me in the right direction.
No matter the chance or choice I make
I know there is a spiritual angel of hope keeping me pro-
tected.

In times of great joy and in times
Of the hardest pain life may throw my way,
I now flip my coin of hope knowing
The right spiritual truth will help me know all will be ok.

CHAPTER 15 - THE DETERMINED SPIRIT NAMED COURAGE

No Matter How Tough Life Gets, We Should Always Keep Trying No Matter How Many Odds are Against Us.

So many times in our lives it would just be easier to give up and quit trying so hard to succeed. There are moments when it seems we will never overcome our limitations because the odds seem too great to endure.

The following poem, "The Determined Spirit Named Courage", is about an experience I had helping my mom find a new kitten. One Saturday morning, I went with my mom and sister to a local animal shelter in my hometown. While we were there, a poor, struggling black and white tuxedo kitten who suffered from back leg paralysis was walking all around the room. I remember just watching how, despite his paralysis, he played with the other cats as if nothing would hold him back. He let me pet him, and as I did, I could feel a surge of warm, compassionate energy resonate within his soul.

I can remember thinking that if this kitten who could barely walk could keep going and maintain a kind, loving demeanor in his tough condition, that I could find the courage to overcome anything as well. Therefore, the poem that follows is a direct result of the inspiration I received from that special kitten within myself I nicknamed Courage.

————————————

The Determined Spirit Named Courage

I was walking around in frustrating circles
In the maze of life trying to find my way.
Somehow I needed to know I was not the only one
Feeling so discouraged some days.

To my surprise I noticed a black and white kitten
Whose back legs were pressed together.
This little kitten seemed to know how to keep the faith
Knowing one day life would get better.

I could not take my eyes off of his weary little legs
No matter how hard I tried.
Seeing him struggle to move around despite
His paralysis made me want to cry.

I walked up to this little kitten feeling

He just needed to know someone loved him so.
He looked up at me with his sparkling green eyes
Hoping I would protect him and not let him go.

I continued to watch him run and play
In the little room he and I called life.
He fell down a few times but he kept going
Reassuring me everything would be all right.

After some time had passed I noticed he seemed
Not to let unexpected surprises bring him down.
It may have taken him a long time to get where he wanted
But he succeeded without losing ground.

I was so amazed at the strength this little kitten had found
In the short time we had met.
Even when I felt lost I could look at him play
Without fear encouraging me not to lose hope just yet.

I sat down in front of my new little friend to pet him
And could hear him purring peacefully.
He connected with my fears within to let me know
He understood the need to experience life gracefully.

I looked deep into his magical eyes feeling a connection
To his spirit determined not to quit.
He sent me some calm, serene energy to help me
Not let life keep giving me such a constant fit.

As my new friend I named Courage watched me
Across the room with such love,

I could sense he wanted me to know God
Was looking out for me just like him from the Heavens
above.

The day I discovered Courage was the moment
My life had become enriched with rhyme and reason.
Now I found my own determined spirit to appreciate
Each chapter of my life with every passing season.

CHAPTER 16 - THE FAITHFUL YELLOW ROSE

In a World Often Torn Apart By Deceptive and False Charms, God Does Send Faithful Friends to Help Encourage Us and Give Us Strength.

In this world, there are constant reminders of broken dreams and false promises. So many people will tell you one thing, yet never keep their word. In fact, it often gets to the point that being able to really trust someone becomes a hardship, because so many people are not what they seem. For most of my life, I was always a very trusting soul. However, getting hurt many times over often left me feeling bitter and unwilling to trust anyone.

The following poem, "The Faithful Yellow Rose", is all about a special flower who is able to help the discouraged spirit of a troubled soul who feels she has nobody she can really trust. In fact, this poem is a reminder to all of us that often when it feels like the whole world has left us in distress, God often sends beautiful signs of His undying mercy. When there is deception, it is so easy to just assume everyone is untrustworthy. However, just like this lovely, yellow rose, there are treasures of kindness that still exist in a world drowning in disillusionment.

———————————————————

The Faithful Yellow Rose

I was not sure why I seemed to always
Get pulled into a world of confusion.
It was as if I had been misled by
Dishonest loyalties drowning under false illusion.

No matter which way I turned and no matter
What language I tried to speak,
My heart was scared to try too hard
Because my spirit felt so weak.

I was thinking back over my past questioning
Why I let others hurt me so.
Then I realized that sometime I needed
To finally let all the bad times go.

Somehow I could not figure out how to overcome
The wounds that kept me feeling down,
But I was determined to stay strong no matter
How much others knocked me around.

So one day I decided I had enough of letting

My past and present struggles throw me off track.
I was determined to let go of the past
And face the future without ever looking back.

In the midst of my decision to take
A new path that I wished to give me hope,
I stumbled across a yellow rose that caught my eye
With such beauty I thought maybe I can cope.

The winds of change and the storms of despair
Still tried to blow my way,
Yet somehow the lovely yellow rose had an aura
That let me know it would all be ok.

I stood in awe of its magical charm because
I felt this yellow rose was meant for me to see and feel.
Standing in its presence I could sense it had been hurt too
And wanted to find a friend that was real.

Sometimes people come and go and sometimes
There are others we need to leave behind.
The more I stared at the yellow rose in all its splendor
The more I realized sometimes life is kind.

I knelt down in front of this sweet yellow rose
Because I felt a close connection I could not explain.
I felt a special bond with her that was so so spiritual
It made my restless spirit feel more tame.

When I whispered to this yellow rose that
I really needed a friend to never leave my side,

She leaned a little closer to me as if to say
I will be here when you need to cry.

I told her that I felt like giving up because
It seemed I was trapped under a world of despair.
She just leaned a little closer and cried
I know how it feels to hurt but I will always care.

I asked her if she could wave a magic wand
To remove all the bad energy that tried to make me sick.
She said just take a smell of my sweet petals
And you will gain the strength to survive life's tricks.

In the middle of all my struggles and
My soul searching to find one true friend I could love,
I wrapped my arms around the admirable yellow rose
Knowing God was smiling from above.

Even though I knew problems would still come
And my worries would still try to make me feel sad,
Knowing God sent me a faithful yellow rose to be
My kindred spirit made my heart feel forever glad.

CHAPTER 17 - THE
GIFT OF LIFE

Life is So Short, and We Should Treasure Every Moment God
Gives Us.

It is often we hear others talk about how short life really is. Right after a tragic moment or an overwhelming problem happens, we immediately look for answers to try and understand why certain events had to happen in the first place. There have been countless times in my life where I questioned God trying to figure out why my life had to turn out a particular way. What I discovered is that I needed to appreciate all the good and bad moments and make the best of my life as much as possible.

The following poem, "The Gift of Life", is a reflection of the brevity of our time on this earth and how every minute of every day should be cherished completely. Life becomes very hectic for each of us and many times it is challenging to find the time we want to tell others how much we care and to embrace every day as if it was our last. I once heard someone say that success is a journey not a destination, and I honestly feel life is journey that we are meant to make the best of along the way.

The Gift of Life

I was looking around for
A way to ease my mind.
It seemed I could never catch a break
From the constant stress of misfortune's crime.

In much despair I looked around
For a place where I could rest,
Yet no matter where I turned
I fell into a world of unrelenting distress.

I decided to take a walk away
From everything I knew to be true.
At some point I wanted to convince myself
There are times when life is good to you.

I got a call one day from a mother
Who loved her daughter so much.
She told me she almost lost her child from
An unpredictable illness that came with a brutal touch.

In a moment when it seemed
I could not make sense of life at all,
I thought about how our lives can change
On a dime making us victims of life's uncertain calls.

In so many ways I was angry
And so wanting to forget.
I just kept the faith that God would
Give me strength to not give up just yet.

When I looked within to try and see
Why life was full of so much surprise,
I then looked above me and saw
A beautiful morning dove come flying by.

With tears in my eyes I begged God to help me
Understand why I was struggling in so many ways.
Then I caught the morning dove sitting on a power line
Right above me with such grace.

My eyes could not seem to leave this special morning dove
Because I felt he was sign of peace.
In the midst of all my worries he seemed
To flap his wings to comfort and put me at ease.

There were tears from my past fears
Just rolling down my cheeks.
I was so broken that even when I tried
To communicate with the dove I could barely speak.

In a moment of complete silence and in a moment
When it seemed everything was falling apart,
I just watched the morning dove perched on a power line
Make its own connection to my heart.

With every breath I took I could feel him

Sending me energy it would all be ok.
It was as if my new little friend knew
I just wanted to run so far away.

After watching my new friend and feeling
The loving energy he would send to heal my soul,
I saw him fly down right before my feet as if
He was determined to not let me go.

In a moment of weakness I really wondered
How would I be able to help my friend now,
Yet no matter how hard life could be,
He flapped his wings as if to say it will get better somehow.

I was desperate for change and eager
To break the chains that seemed to tear me down.
No matter where life took me I knew
My new friend the morning dove would always be around.

As I moved on from the place where
It seemed time just stood still,
The morning dove flew above me as if
He promised to surround me with a love that's real.

Looking back I could see so many crazy things
I never understood and needed to leave behind.
As I kept moving forward, I felt God sent my new friend
To help me make sense of life this time.

During rainy days and moments when the sun
Just kept shining the morning dove never left me alone.

We now shared a mutual appreciation for the gift of life
And found a place our hearts could call home.

CHAPTER 18 - THE GOLDEN KEY OF FREEDOM THAT CHANGED MY LIFE

God Wants to Set Us Free From Heartache and Misery So We Can Rise Above Our Troubles to Embrace Happier Ways of Life.

I must admit I am truly a free spirit and have lived my life in a very unconventional way. Having my freedom to dream, explore, and take adventures in life has always been important to me. Unfortunately, there will always be someone or something to try and keep us from being all God wants us to be. However, I have learned that God does not intend for us to feel miserable and trapped in a life that does not embrace our destiny.

The following poem, "The Golden Key of Freedom that Changed My Life", is all about finding that special key to unlock an authentic life where justice and truth exist. Restriction from being who we are meant to be and from living the happy life God intends I feel is a real tragedy. I made a decision a long time ago not to compromise who I am or what I want just to please someone else. If there is one thing I learned early in my life, it is to share the key of freedom with others seeking to find the path where they can be true to their hopes and dreams.

The Golden Key of Freedom that Changed My Life

I was searching high and low
For the answers to a better way of life.
No matter how much I tried to make it happen
I got frustrated with my failed efforts every time.

I prayed and asked God one night to send me something
I could use to improve my fate.
Much to my surprise the next morning
I found a golden key that seemed to have something to say.

I held the key up to my head because
I felt I needed something to free my mind.
It was as if this golden key could unlock
The door to my brain that seemed frozen in time.

When I looked within my mind to understand
Why I felt I had to please everyone but me,
I realized the key I held in my hand could
Give me a freedom I needed so desperately.

I unlocked all the fears that kept my mind trapped
In thinking I had to conform to others expectations.
When I looked at how much I made others happy,
My mind became trapped under chains of desolation.

I took this golden key and unlocked the chains
That kept my mind playing tricks on my soul.
I had finally gotten to the point I needed
To set my mind free so I could let all my fears go.

After this special golden key freed my mind
Of years of being trapped in despair,
I realized I needed to unlock my weary heart
That had been broken by those who did not care.

I took a journey into my heart to see if
I could find the reason I always held back.
Somehow I needed to unlock the chains around
My heart that needed a true friend to keep me on track.

I went a little deeper inside my heart to see
Why real love had been so hard for me to find.
Then I used the key in my hand to free my heart
So I could take more chances this time.

After unlocking the door to my heart that
Had been wounded by years of regret and worry,
I realized the golden key was God's way of saying
I deserved to be happy and create a new life story.

Now that I had used the golden key of freedom

To free my mind and my heart,
I decided to use the key to unlock the prison
That kept my free spirit struggling in the dark.

All my life I knew I had a vision of creativity
And an imaginative soul that was meant to be free.
I never could understand those that lived in a box
Based on what the world wanted them to be.

When I remembered all the times I wanted
To take risks to make my dreams come true,
I could see the times my spirit remained suppressed
By insecurities keeping me lost and feeling blue.

As I journeyed deeper into my inner spirit,
I was shocked at how broken promises had kept it in prison.
I knew it was time to take the golden key I cherished
To give my spirit a new meaningful vision.

As I unlocked the lock around
My chained spirit to finally set it free,
I could feel a joy rise up inside because
I had conquered so many years of misery.

This golden key of freedom was a true miracle
From God that helped change my life.
After setting free my mind, heart, and spirit
I could now dream of happier times to come every night.

CHAPTER 19 - THE HEART THAT WOULD NOT QUIT

God's Unconditional Love Will Keep Us Strong and in Times When It Seems Nobody Cares, He Sends Another Caring Soul Our Way to Let Us Know We Are Never Alone.

Sometimes I thought it would be so much easier to quit trying than to keep trying and face one disappointment after the next. I can honestly say there have been many times I felt like I was just going through the motions of life as if I was only half living instead of enjoying life completely. In fact, I feel that is how so many people feel because life is not always the fun adventure we seek. Even when times are hard, it often feels like nobody truly understands. However, I have learned that there is always at least one person God sends into our lives who can empathize with our pain and sorrows.

The following poem, "The Heart that Would Not Quit", is about one dejected soul who feels as if she is lost in a world of despair. She feels alone and as if is nobody really cares until she meets another kindred spirit of sorts who understands her feelings and develops a special way of connecting to her heart and soul. Despite her desire to give up, the lost soul soon realizes God has sent a true friend who will stand by her side no matter what.

The Heart that Would Not Quit

There were so many moments that
My life had been so sad and stressful.
I remember getting down on my hands and knees
Praying for a time that was more restful.

I often closed my eyes and
Made my most hopeful wish.
Somehow I trusted God would
Lead me on a new path to surpass life's tests.

Many times I felt as if maybe love
Was for someone else to truly feel.
I wondered how long it would take for me
To discover a heart of spiritual love that was real.

Through so many half-hearted love affairs
And times where the love was just one sided,
I prayed that somehow the right love I needed
Would give me strength and keep me guided.

I walked around just holding my hand
Over my most desperate heart.
It seemed as hard as my life had been
God was giving me a fresh new start.

Then I found myself walking right into a room
Where I felt a special connection had begun.
There was something so sweet about the way I felt
As if the right love had now come.

My heart just kept beating
With such a mystical pleasure.
There was great love in the air
That was as sweet as a magical treasure.

From another place and time this love
Was unlike most people had endured.
It had the essence of joy and an undying hope
That was strong and forever pure.

I often experienced this loving connection
That was God's precious gift to me.
I could look right into the eyes of the other half of my soul
Who held the key to my spiritual destiny.

Many times I struggled to tell the one
Who shared my soul just how much I cared.
I hoped my smiles and encouraging words
Would be a sign that my heart was always there.

There were days that I had worked so hard

And felt I could barely catch my breath.
Then all I had to do was look at my kindred spirit
Whose eyes could heal my soul with such depth.

In times of my greatest weakness
When it seemed I could not go on,
All my kindred spirit had to do was
Smile at me to put an end to my soul's sad songs.

In times when it felt I was so on
Top of the world and feeling so strong,
I could feel your magical spirit transforming
My soul and helping me forgive other people's wrongs.

Even when I wanted to give the
Other half of my soul my entire heart,
It was as if there was an understanding that
The time would come when we would not be apart.

It is amazing how time goes by and
Yet my heart will never ever quit.
The love I feel for my kindred spirit
Keeps it beating with such passion and wit.

Now when I hold my hand over my heart
All through the day and night,
I can feel the precious love of my soul mate
Giving me faith that everything will turn out right.

CHAPTER 20 - THE JOURNEY OF THE HEART

Sometimes We Have to Go Through a Sea of Restless Energy to Understand that Heartbreaks Happen for a Reason and New Beginnings Await Us if We Keep the Faith.

The heart has always been a mystery to me. Sometimes the feelings I have felt have made great sense to me, and other times I could not understand why I felt the way I did and how I could keep holding on to feelings I needed to release. I have also learned that the heart wants what the heart wants, and even if there is heartbreak, it is often meant for us to feel highs and lows in order to undergo true spiritual growth. I believe we are meant to experience shades of love, and each love we feel teaches us something new about who we are and what we want out of life.

The following poem, "The Journey of the Heart", is a poem about the wounds of a broken heart and the need to find answers to the pain. It is a reflection of how one soul

85

is in need of hope and healing to learn from broken relationships from the past in order to embrace a new chapter of love. As I have discovered, it is good to feel love at many levels to help us appreciate that true spiritual love never dies.

———————————————

The Journey of the Heart

I was lost and confused feeling as if my heart
Remained broken from years of distress.
I was just praying somehow that God
Would set me free from all my restlessness.

I spent hours on end praying for the
Chains around me to somehow be broken.
It seemed no matter how long or hard
I searched for answers some words would be left unspoken.

The years in my life have rolled by
Without anything solid to ground my heart.
It seems all the almost love stories I had
Left me feeling sad and completely torn apart.

Somehow I managed to play the part
Of the kind of girl who has it all together,
Yet underneath it all I remain a chaotic soul
Trying to find my way through stormy weather.

There are times I often feel I will never
Find the answers to why love has been just out of reach.

It seemed the more I tried to make others love me
The more my heart remained wounded and weak.

As time has progressed I have found that
My heart has always been in a struggle to find a way out.
I feel I am looking from the inside of a prison
Of doubt where all I wanna do is just shout.

If I could just break the chains that have
Kept my heart so troubled and confused,
Maybe I could find the strength to have hope again
And know love exists for those who remain true.

I am not sure how long my journey through
The wilderness of lost dreams will last.
All I know are the memories that exist within me
Give me strength to cherish the past.

Sometimes I feel I will never be able to get past
All the mistakes I made with those loved and lost.
It seems the chances I took felt right at the time
Yet the lessons learned came at the highest cost.

I look back at my past and wonder why God
Led me down so many paths I could not understand.
Then when I thought of every memory
I realized the detours were meant to give me strength again.

Looking back and moving forward are
Not always the easiest moves to make.

I find myself drowning in despair over all
The bad choices I made and my present mistakes.

So many times I have wished I could just run away
And start a fresh new chapter in my life.
Maybe God would give me the chance I needed
To make new choices that would be better this time.

I feel like a lost sailboat on the ocean
Just tossed in so many directions.
It seems the more I try to remain grounded
My heart grows sick again from fear of rejection.

I often feel like a bird just flying in the air
Hoping I can set my imprisoned heart free.
Then I just fall flat to the ground with broken wings
That have been suffocated in misery.

I know God has a reason for all the
Ups and downs in matters of the heart we face.
Even when things are great there will come times
The lows will be where we learn to walk in grace.

My heart and soul constantly remind my mind
To not give up that love is all that really matters.
In a world where chaos reigns God offers a love
Without limits that survives all the hopeless chatter.

If I could just convince my mind that
My heart really has a few stories to tell,

My heart would say I may have loved too much,
But it made me feel good and kept me feeling well.

If I could just convince my heart to be
More careful in how I share how I feel,
Then maybe I could soothe the restless matters
In my heart with a love that is finally real.

CHAPTER 21 - THE LEOPARD THAT COULD NOT CHANGE ITS SPOTS

We Must Accept Our Strengths and Weaknesses and Be True to Ourselves.

One of my all time favorite sayings is that a leopard cannot change its spots. For the longest time, I have always associated this saying with negative energy. However, I decided to think of it in a more positive way. After all, if a leopard has good qualities why change them?

The following poem, "The Leopard that Could Not Change His Spots", is about someone who meets an interesting leopard whose spots hold great spiritual wisdom. Through the friendship that develops between the leopard and the searching soul, great spiritual truths are revealed. The best part of it all is that the soul seeker in the poem learns to be more true to himself and to accept the things in life he cannot change.

The Leopard that Could Not Change His Spots

I was chasing a leopard and
Demanded to know his name.
He just laughed at me and said
See if you can catch me and keep me tame.

I was doubtful to follow him because
I was not sure if I could trust him so.
He just smiled at me and said come walk with me
And I will protect your soul.

He took me into a valley far away
From everything I had known.
I was fearful to take the jump but
I knew sometimes you have to leave home.

He said one of my spots has been full of bad choices
From the past I wish I could forget,
Yet I've learned not to run away from my mistakes
And learn to face all of my regrets.

As we walked further the leopard showed me
Another spot that had been tainted with loss.
When I asked why the spot felt so heavy
He said there were times I felt like a lost cause.

Curious to understand the next spot
He showed me that was warm as could be,
He just sighed loudly and said I have learned
Not to let life get the best of me.

After climbing out of the valley he showed me
Another spot that was soft to the touch.
When we managed to get back to the top
He just whispered I often love too much.

As we lay in a meadow marked by
The most exquisite flowers all around,
The leopard showed me a colorful spot
Encouraging me hope would soon be found.

One by one he revealed each spot that had
A life lesson and a story waiting to be told.
He said trust me I have been hurt enough
And know what it is like to left out in the cold.

After the last spot was revealed I asked my friend
If there was a chance I had missed one of his spots.
I told him I really liked the way he protected me
And the faithful ways he loved me a lot.

I followed my new friend to the top of a mountain
Where he showed me two spots connected.
He said I want you to know these spots are the reminder
I will keep you safe so you never feel rejected.

CHAPTER 22 - THE LIGHT AT THE END OF A DARK TUNNEL

Even When It Seems Life is Totally Hopeless We Have to Keep the Faith that God Will Provide a Better, Happier Way As Long As We Don't Lose Heart.

If there is one thing I have learned over the course of my life, it is to trust that there really is a light at the end of a dark tunnel. There have been countless times I have felt trapped in darkness as if I had no way to turn. I spent most of my past running away from facing my fears because I felt it would be way too much for me to handle.

However, all my running from fear just kept me spiraling down a staircase of despair until I finally realized that I had to trust God would lead me on the right path. Learning to trust God when times are hard is not easy for any of us because we live in a society of instant gratification. Instead of patiently waiting for the bad times to pass, we often want to live in a time of constant peace. Even though a peaceful life is what we all desire, I have learned my greatest spiritual growth came during times of frustration and pain. I had to struggle in order to grow stronger and better.

In the following poem, "The Light at the End of a Dark Tunnel", the story is told of a journey of a lost soul trying to find his way out of darkness to a place where the light of serenity shines through boldly and strongly.

=================================

The Light at the End of A Dark Tunnel

I was walking along through a tunnel
Full of darkness and cold air.
I was so mad at life and asked God why
Some people were so selfish and did not care.

Somehow I felt that I had been punished
To spend my life walking around this tunnel in vain.
Then I realized that maybe I had to spend
Some time in the darkness to come to terms with my pain.

In the midst of my despair I just felt
So trapped as if I could not see.
Then I just kept searching endlessly
For something encouraging to set me free.

I kept looking around and did not see anything
But dark energies trying to bring me down.

It seemed the more I tried to figure things out
I remained confused and lost within a constant frown.

With little strength left I just decided
To fall down on my weary knees.
I decided to say a prayer in the depths of my loneliness
That God would come rescue me.

With little breath I had
Within my soul to fully breathe,
I prayed and asked God to give me the answers
To come to terms with all my miseries.

I listened intently for God to somehow
Give me the solution to all of my constant worries,
Yet the harder I tried to hear His response
I was too busy replaying all my crazy, troubled stories.

There were voices from my past echoing
Words of constant defeat in my ears.
All it did was remind me of all the times
I felt like a lost soul suffocating from my continual fears.

When I reflected back upon my past wounds
And all the crazy setbacks that kept me feeling cold,
I could still feel the chills of wrong choices
And bad decisions making me feel so completely old.

It seemed the harder I tried to understand
The lessons that I was meant to understand,

I prayed that God would help me find a new path
Where I would never let go of His hand.

As the tears of past bad choices seemed
To flood my memory with years of regret,
There came a soft, gentle voice that spoke to me
In the dark tunnel saying don't give up just yet.

It was as if I had almost stopped hoping
That things would get better,
Yet the sweet spirit of God reassured me
He and I would always be together.

With much desperate hope to find the courage
To begin a new path that was truly full of peace,
I could hear the special, kind words of God whispering
Just have faith and keep holding on to me.

Knowing that I had not always listened to
His voice in my past like I should have done,
God breathed a fresh vision within my dying spirit
To comfort me that a great path had just begun.

With more courage and a bolder hope that maybe
I could find a way out of the dark night of my soul,
I may have been walking in the dark but now
Had felt a love so much that would never let me go.

Even though the world around me was so dark
And full of possible threats and rejection,

I held on to the words of God that He would
Be my refuge and keep me going in the right direction.

After many long days and nights of walking
In such a dark and dreary place,
I noticed a light ahead of me that seemed to shine
On the path before me with such elegance and grace.

Through all my prayers and determination
To keep the faith no matter how bad things may be,
When I reached the light at the end of my dark tunnel,
I thanked God for loving my soul relentlessly.

CHAPTER 23 - THE LUCKY COIN AND A DESTINED PATH

Good Luck Often Comes in the Most Unexpected Places, and We Should Trust that Divine Intervention Leads Us Down the Right Path.

Throughout my life, I have always believed everyone should have a good luck charm. Sometimes such charms can come to us in ways we did not expect. However, the blessings we receive are very special. I really feel God sends us divine messages through special objects at times which is why when I feel drawn to certain things I usually feel led to explore my discoveries as much as possible.

The following poem, "The Lucky Coin and a Destined Path", is all about one person who is down on her luck. As she travels down what she hopes is a new path, she stumbles across a coin that becomes her good luck charm to believe good things await her if she does not give up.

The Lucky Coin and a Destined Path

I was walking down a path that
I chose to take all on my own.
It was much different than anything
I had ever experienced and took me far from home.

There was a spiritual desire inside
To embrace a life where I could feel free.
I was sick and tired of letting others
Always get the best of me.

I had lived everyday from
The outside looking in.
It seemed everyone else had found
True happiness yet I knew I had to find it within.

Despite my frustration at all the moments
In my life I had let pass,
I asked God how long my sadness
And upsets were gonna last.

In the midst of my confusion the answer
Never seemed to come to mind,
Yet I was determined to walk this new path
And find a life where I could be true to myself this time.

I stumbled across this shining gold coin
That I felt led to pick up.

Somehow there was an energy inside it
Crying out keep the faith because you are good enough.

I held this beautiful gold coin
In the palm of my weary hand.
Tears were streaming down my face because
I felt God had sent me a friend that did understand.

I sat down on a rock on the side of my new path
Watching the sun reflect its light on this coin.
When I was too tired to keep going the strength
Of it in my hands said you will survive every storm.

I tossed the coin in the air wondering
If it would land on good luck.
When I looked over to the side of me it had fallen
Within the petals of a daisy flower full of great love.

I watched this daisy support this gold coin
Even though it felt heavy and ready to fall.
The daisy radiated the kind of serene energy
That said life is hard but you can climb over any wall.

I took the gold coin in my hand hoping that
It would bring me some greater luck.
Then a yellow butterfly flew my way and moved
The coin around so I would not feel so stuck.

I was crying with great relief because
I knew I really needed a change.

So I tossed this gold coin in the air asking God
To direct us both where destiny could finally feel sane.

In a matter of moments all the clouds
And rocks in my path seemed to disappear.
The sun was shining brightly as if to say
Your fate is not far from here.

As I walked down the path I was not sure
Where it would take me or even how far I should go.
The lucky coin I now carry called destiny was
The friend breathing new energy into my soul.

CHAPTER 24 - THE MAGICAL 8 BALL

God Often Sends Us Answers to Life's Most Challenging Questions in Curious But Puzzling Ways, Yet If We Listen Closely We Will Find The Answers We Seek.

When I was a child, I remember getting a most fascinating gift. It was called a Magical 8 Ball. The whole purpose of this ball was to ask it a question, shake it up, and then wait for the desired answer to surface. What I found so interesting is that it was like this black ball sensed I needed answers. Looking back I honestly feel maybe God used this device to help lead me in the right direction.

In my adult life, I often think how good it would be if I still had that black ball where I could pose all my questions and hope for the right answers to come. Now with the advances of modern technology I have discovered that there are plenty of electronic devices that will allow you to ask a question leading you to the right answers.

In the following poem, "The Magical 8 Ball", a poetic

story is told of a young woman who received a mysterious
gift at her door. What she discovers is this Magical 8 Ball
becomes a way for her to find solutions to her problems
with the help of spiritual intervention along the way.

The Magical 8 Ball

On a warm spring evening I heard a knock
At my door in the middle of the night,
And I wondered who on earth could it be
And if everything was all right.

Curious to see who was on
The other side of my door,
When I opened up to see
There was a gift for me to explore.

Somewhat scared but ready to open this gift
That caught me by surprise,
When I opened the package I looked and
Saw a black little 8 ball with several messages inside.

I was not sure who would have brought me
This gift at such an odd time,
Yet something inside said an angel is trying
To help you make sense of your life this time.

As I went inside I first asked the 8 ball
Where I could find a place of complete peace?

The answer came "can't predict now" so I realized
Maybe I had to look within to find a calm release.

The second question that came to my mind was
Why did I always feel I was not good enough?
The answer came "my reply is no" so I realized
I needed to feel more confident and be tough.

The third question I raised was why does
Everyone else seem so much happier than me?
The answer came "my sources say no" because
Life on the outside is not always what it may seem.

The fourth question I asked was I meant
To go through so many years of struggle and pain?
The answer came "as I see it, yes" because you have
To go through trials to protect your good name.

The fifth question I asked was I meant to suffer this long
To learn what God wanted me to know?
The answer came "most likely" to keep the faith
And have wisdom to grow.

The sixth question I asked was why I seemed
To give so much and always feel so drained?
The answer came "better not tell you now"
So I could find courage to stay strong without any shame.

The seventh question I asked was why could
I not heal the wounds of all for whom I cared?

The answer came "don't count on it" because
Some have to learn that life is not always fair.

The eighth question I asked was why did it
Take my broken heart so long to heal?
The answer came "without a doubt" I was meant
To make mistakes so I could learn to trust God's will.

The ninth question I asked was when
Would I stop feeling pulled in so many directions?
The answer came "ask again later" when I had learned
That all happens for a reason with good lessons.

The last question I asked was why it took me
So long to trust my heart and quit controlling my mind.
The answer came "it is certain" I was meant to know
Love conquers all through the course of time.

CHAPTER 25 - THE MESSENGER BIRD FROM GOD

God Speaks to Our Souls Through Nature, and We Should Listen Closely to the Spiritual Wisdom Nature's Finest Creatures Can Bring to Us.

I have always loved morning doves. In fact, I often am amazed at their simple beauty when they are sitting upon power lines or on rooftops. Every time I see one of these birds I feel they have a calming effect on my often restless soul. In fact, I feel morning doves carry spiritual messages from God of true peace.

I wrote the following poem, "The Messenger Dove from God", based on my personal love and inspiration I have received from morning doves. So many times when I have been feeling down and out I can look above me outside and see one of these precious doves. Each time I see one of these birds I often feel a calm, healing energy come

over me as if God is letting me know He is always there and
that He will never leave my side.

The Messenger Dove from God

Frustrated and hurt I just kept
Wishing that somebody could understand.
I was hopeless and crushed by another disappointment
That left me feeling unbalanced again.

Somehow I needed God to help me know
That the pain would somehow pass.
I kept looking for a sign of hope that
My sadness would not last.

As I looked upon the rooftop
Of the place I called home,
There was a precious dove that greeted me
So I would not feel all alone.

I looked into the eyes of this beautiful dove
That just seemed to radiate peace.
Its little eyes pierced through the darkness of my soul
With a calm, restful release.

I just could not seem to take my eyes off
This little dove perched upon my rooftop.
It flapped its wings a few times as if to say
Have faith and your heartache will soon stop.

As I kept staring at this little dove that seemed
To have a message for me this day,
It was like I could hear the voice of God
Whisper through his soul that everything would be ok.

I had been so upset thinking why I let myself
Be hurt and overcome with despair,
Yet the little dove gently flew closer to say
I will help you fly high again because God cares.

I felt taken with this dove because I sensed
He was meant to catch my eye.
In a moment of silence it connected with my spirit
As if to say stay strong and I would survive.

As I began to walk into my home to
Get some much needed rest,
I smiled at this spiritual dove just to say thank you
For giving me a break from my distress.

When I looked out my window I noticed
The dove was flying close by.
My weary soul found comfort knowing
This was God's messenger destined to stay by my side.

CHAPTER 26 - THE MIRACLE I PRAYED FOR

Miracles Can Happen When We Least Expect Them Turning Our World Around in The Most Positive Direction.

All my life I have felt like I was on the outside looking in. In fact, I have spent so much of my life feeling like every obstacle under the moon and stars was trying to block me from my dreams. Time and time again I have found myself completely discouraged and wondering if things would ever get better.

Despite all the roadblocks I have encountered in my life, I have also been reminded of the simple things God has done for me. I do know that being able to stand strong when all the odds have been against me has been God's way of helping me discover the beauty in life. It is so easy to see darkness rather than light when times are challenging, yet I have learned that God is always in control. Just

when we think things can't get better God makes us realize
He is always there for us.

In the following poem, "The Miracle I Prayed For", the
story is about feeling overwhelmed with life, yet there is
evidence that new beginnings are possible always.

The Miracle I Prayed For

God knows how much I have
Wanted to be set free from it all,
Yet as hard as I have tried to remove all my obstacles
All I ever did was completely fall.

Time and time again I wondered what it would
Take to escape the prison of negative vibes,
And yet somehow God could hear my cry for help
Underneath my ever fading smiles.

During every moment I have questioned
Everything that has happened to me,
I knew there would have to come a time
I could embrace a better destiny.

The rains of misfortune have always
Been so in love with my soul,
Yet my heart never felt the same and was
Determined to let this bitter enemy go.

I was so tired of trying to fit into a world
Where I realized I would never belong.
No matter what anyone else thought I knew belonging
To the spiritual world was my forever love song.

Everyday I could see birds hanging from my feeders
Trying to get the food they needed to survive.
They seemed to understand the struggles that
Had kept me trapped in a world of unanswered whys.

Everywhere I looked I could see butterflies
All around my questioning heart.
They sensed I was tired of being the strong one
And needed a good friend to keep me from falling apart.

Through the shadows around me I felt lives
Who passed before me trying to help me out.
I could seem as calm as a sunset on the outside
But my inner fears made me just want to shout.

Throughout my life there have always been
People around me who felt they knew me well,
Yet on the surface I appear to have it together
When inside I often feel trapped by other people's hell.

Years have passed and I feel as if I have
Always been on the outside looking in.
When I compare my life to others I realize
I was not meant to know what might have been.

There are some who walk roads where

The highway ends in great fortune and fame.
Then there are others like me who are always
Fighting to reach their dreams feeling lost and ashamed.

The funny thing is I know now my own struggles
Are helping me help others feel better.
Just when nobody understands God sends a sunrise
To let me know I will never be a forgotten treasure.

Most people don't believe in miracles
Because they lose their faith in life,
Yet on the inside I know God is the only one
That can make the bad times turn out all right.

I am a dreamer of love and feel so many people
Lose sight of what it really means.
In the spiritual world in which I live I believe
In kindred spirits who understand the power of a dream.

Love is the forever mystery that so many
Search the world over to really truly feel.
In the midst of this life there are soul mates
Who are linked to each other by a love that is always real.

I wish had the answers for why some days
I feel I can conquer everything that brings me down
Because I believe in the power of kindred souls who
Speak a language of love that is always around.

I believe in the miracle that God promised to
Give you and me from the time we were born.

He said one day you will find a love like
No other that will keep your heart forever warm.

I believe in the miracle I have prayed for
That has come to take my soul by surprise.
All I have to do is trust in the power of change
And believe the love among kindred spirits never dies.

CHAPTER 27 - THE MOMENT I DECIDED NOT TO LET LIFE PASS ME BY

We Must Make Every Moment of Life Count Because We Never Know What Might Happen To Keep Us From Enjoying It.

I feel we all spend most of our time looking out the window of our existence wondering if there is much more to life than what we presently are experiencing. As we get older, it is so easy to look back and wonder why we did not try to be more and do more. The regrets from past mistakes can begin to overwhelm us so much that it feels like life can become way too much for us to handle.

In the following poem, "The Moment I Decided Not to Let Life Pass Me By", the story is told of one person's sadness who feels she has not made the most of her life. In this poem, she feels as if everyone around her is happy, yet as she watches life happen while she remains trapped in a world of lost dreams, she realizes that something has to change. What she discovers is that as she reaches the breaking point and can no longer stand by on the sidelines of her life, she makes a bold decision that she will not let life pass her by.

The Moment I Decided Not to Let Life Pass Me By

One moment I was faced with cars passing so fast
Around me I wondered when they would stop.
No matter where I looked I felt like
I was on a race track that rushed my spirit quite a lot.

I felt like I had been standing beside
A highway full of twists and turns.
Somewhere within I wondered when I would
Ever quit letting life happen and keep striving to learn.

The next moment I was sitting on a park bench
Watching sweet children play without fear.
As a smile came upon my face I realized
They knew how to have fun without shedding a tear.

I was thinking to myself back to the time
When I was child feeling strong and free.
I realized those were the times I enjoyed life
So much without the stress and misery.

In another moment I was sitting beside
An ocean watching the waves crash on the shore.

I watched dolphins swimming in the sea
Learning to discover the special treats life has in store.

Watching these beautiful animals along with
The seagulls that flew high in the sky
Made me realize God wanted me to take time
To enjoy the simple things without asking why.

In my next moment I was sitting in a
Shopping mall watching people come and go.
When each person passed I could feel their energy
Whisper messages to me I was meant to know.

I was not sure what I was meant to learn
But I sensed some of these people had lost their joy.
So in a moment of concern I clutched my spiritual necklace
For protection as my most treasured toy.

In the next moment of my life I was sitting
On a raft alone in the middle of a crowded lake.
There were boats speeding around me as if
They could care less if they made a mistake.

It reminded me of the times I made
So many choices without considering the danger.
I could feel chills run down my spine as I remember
Feeling so alone like a wandering stranger.

In the last moment I recall falling
Fast asleep deep into a dream.

I was greeted by those I had loved and lost
Who whispered life is not always what it seems.

There were memories from times past
And future predictions this dream brought my way.
I knew eventually I would wake up and must
Take the lessons I learned to face a brand new day.

After all of these unique moments in my life
And with so many I had yet to endure.
I knew in my heart I wanted to keep walking
A more hopeful, spiritual path for sure.

This was the moment I finally decided
To not let my life pass me by.
Even though it might not always be easy to accomplish,
My heart and spirit would always try.

CHAPTER 28 - THE MUCH NEEDED TASTE OF FREEDOM

Even When We Have Been Hurt, We Must Be Willing to Let Go of the Past and Move Forward to Embrace New Beginnings in Our Lives.

Let's face it. Life is often full of heartaches. I guess you could say I have had my heart broken so many times by people or situations that at the time I thought were good for me. However, over the course of time, I realized that I could not keep holding on to angry feelings as they would eventually destroy my spirit. There have been times I wondered why I let others try to control me or have me conform to their ways of acting and thinking. I finally got to the point when I knew it was time to break unhealthy cycles in my life.

The following poem, "The Much Needed Taste of Freedom", is all about one person's struggle to free herself from toxic people and destructive relationships in order to have a life of more freedom. I used to think it was impossible to escape negative people and bad situations, but now I know with enough determination and willpower anything is possible. The key to overcoming bad karma is all in the way we think about it. If we choose to let it into our lives, it could almost destroy us, but if we choose to think positive that we can make our path in life happier, all things are possible.

The Much Needed Taste of Freedom

I was looking for a way
Out of all my distress.
Even though the answer came slowly,
I was blinded by constant stress.

I could never see there was someone holding
On to me so tightly who would just not let me go.
Now that I see what was holding me back
I can find the strength to finally go with the flow.

I could never understand why I let someone
Try to control every aspect of my mind.
Now I see I was being controlled to the point
Where I was running out of time.

I searched within my heart to figure out
Why my life seemed one obstacle after the other.

But what was going on is someone in my life
Too long controlling me like a jealous lover.

I was not really sure what to do to break the cycle
Of someone who wanted to tell my heart what to do.
Every time I tried to move away I would get
Pulled back into the petty cries of I am the best for you.

It was an unhealthy game being played upon
My heart that had been broken way too much.
Now I know that I was a victim of someone
Who used me to fulfill quite a selfish touch.

I'm not sure what the past holds for me in
Terms of the lessons I should have learned,
But I have learned that nobody should control
Your heart and mind because you will get burned.

I wish I had seen deep in my past that I should have
Gotten off the path of confusion quicker,
Yet somehow I was addicted to the need for approval
Making my heart so much sicker.

It is funny how you look back and realize that
Freedom really does not come at a price.
The more you let go of the people hurting you,
The more you realize true feelings are always nice.

I once was sad and upset because I could not see
Why I let someone hurt me by manipulation.

No wonder my spirit was drained so negatively
By a hungry soul lost in a sea of desperation.

I have needed a weight to be lifted that
Has been so hard for me to endure.
It's like God said I know you need some help
So your heart can finally feel pure.

Uncertain of what to do or where to turn
To set the chains free around my heart.
I still pray for God to give me
A much needed, brand new fresh start.

I believe in miracles and I believe one day God leads us
To the kindred soul who will love us forever.
Even if you have to give up what is not good for you
It will lead to a much better treasure.

Now when the storms of life try to blow around
My soul to the point to of it being broken down,
I have to keep the faith that at some point
The hard times will give way to more peaceful sounds.

CHAPTER 29 - THE MYSTERIOUS CLOCK THAT RACES THROUGH TIME

Even Though Time Seems to Go By Fast, We Cannot Change All the Things We Were Meant to Learn Along the Way and Must Be Grateful That God Gives Us a Chance to Embrace a New Destiny for Ourselves.

I have often heard the cliche regarding how fast time flies, and over the course of my life, I have known that to always be true. It seems when there are great moments that they can pass so quickly while the more negative times seem to linger way too long. What I discovered is that no matter what has happened in the past we cannot change it. However, we can make the most of every moment we live.

The following poem, "The Mysterious Clock the Races Through Time", is actually based on a real alarm clock I have on my nightstand right beside my bed. This clock is quite interesting because no matter how I try to set it back to match up with the other clocks in my home, the faster it keeps racing ahead. It is always a reminder to me of how we spend so much of our lives rushing from one moment to the next and encourages me to slow down when life becomes a little too crazy.

The Mysterious Clock that Races Through Time

I kept waking up to a clock that
Seemed to always race through time.
I thought maybe I should set it back
A few minutes and enjoy a lot more of my life.

Instead I decided to embrace the fact that
There are some things I cannot change.
I realized that I was meant to learn from my past
And move on again with hope attached to my name.

The more I tried to rewind the clock I was
Reminded of times I wished I never had learned.
Even though I knew I had to face the fact that
We all must endure hard moments when it is our turn.

With every hour and minute I tried to go
Back to the times when life felt so good,
Yet I knew deep down those times had past
And I had to create new memories the best I could.

Before I knew it this clock was racing hours
And minutes so far ahead where I wanted to be.
It was like I could hear God whisper hang on to Me
When life passes by so fast like a good story.

Frustrated and confused because I really
Wanted to embrace a new hope for tomorrow.
The clock just raced ahead to say don't be afraid
To take risks or you will face great sorrow.

Day and night I wondered if this fast
Moving clock would ever slow down.
I lie in bed at night asking God to give me the strength
To be strong when I just wanted to leave town.

Somehow it felt like my constant struggle
To survive the storms of life would never end.
No matter how fast the clock kept ticking I knew
God would give me the courage to keep trying again.

Every night I thought maybe I can wish for
This clock to just give me a break from my stress.
I could feel it whisper I want you to hurry and
Fall asleep so your dreams will bring you rest.

No matter where I go or what I do to try
And find a way to slow down this clock,
I know the hours and minutes that passed by
Were meant to teach my heart to be tough no matter what.

It is funny how I quit trying to adjust this

Mysterious clock back to the place I desire.
Whether I go back or move forward I realize
This time it is my destiny to succeed that will never expire.

CHAPTER 30 - THE OCEAN OF GOOD FORTUNE

We Create Our Own Good Fortune in Life By Really Allowing Our Hearts and Souls to Connect With the Beauty of Nature Knowing That Life Is Not Always As Bad As it Seems.

I honestly love the beach. For as long as I can remember, I have loved walking along the shore letting the waves crash over my feet. I love watching the seagulls fly peacefully through the air as if they have no worries in the world. There is something about the beach that has always had a calming effect on my often restless spirit.

On one of my beach trips, I wrote the following poem, "The Ocean of Good Fortune" because I realized that no matter how frustrating certain things may be in my life that I could find beauty in the midst of my struggles. It made me realize that sometimes it takes a journey to a place of true healing to get our distressed energies back on the right track.

The Ocean of Good Fortune

I was walking along the shore of a serene beach
With waves crashing back and forth.
Somewhere in my heart I could sense this ocean
Had some secrets I could not ignore.

I stumbled across an array of sand dollars
That just gathered around my weary feet.
It was if they wanted me to know they had survived
Rough waters too and overcame much deceit.

The further I walked I noticed there were
Seagulls of all sizes standing all around.
The more I watched them walk in the sand
I knew they had learned how to stand their ground.

When I looked up into the sky I noticed
a flock of pelicans flying together in harmony.
Somewhere in the midst of their journey
I felt they held the keys to a happier destiny.

I walked a little deeper into the cool waters
As the waves became fierce with great passion.
With each wave that caressed my feet I knew these waters
Took great risks to create positive reactions.

As I took a deep breath my spirit was refreshed
With a warm, gentle breeze from the healing sea.

I knew that no matter how tough life became
God would always be good to me.

The winds of change were blowing all
Around me as the sun began to set.
When I looked up into the sky the colorful rays
Of light reminded me to not give up just yet.

After walking for some time on an ocean shore
That I felt could bring me some peace of mind,
In a few quiet moments I kept the faith
I could overcome my problems this time.

I spent much time feeling drawn to this ocean
That I felt held secret treasures for me to uncover.
Everywhere I felt led to go I knew I needed
To stay open for what my soul longed to discover.

In this ocean of good fortune I was so
Hoping my luck would continue to get better.
I knew God gave me a fresh start to find
The happiness my heart could always treasure.

CHAPTER 31 - THE PROMISING SUN IN THE MIDST OF CLOUDY SKIES

When It Seems Like Everything In Our Lives Is Falling Apart, God Will Often Send Rays of Sunlight Just To Help Us See Hope and Promise Even When The Rest of World is Drowning in Doom and Gloom.

Nothing frustrates me more than to be surrounded by negative people. I know we all have good and bad days, but there are some people who like to spend their lives just being grumpy as if the whole world has disadvantaged them. If I know I am going to be in the company of people like this, I will usually turn the other direction. I know that even when it seems life is totally chaotic that things always get better. If we always see the clouds in life then we will never learn to appreciate those beautiful days when the sun is shining ever so brightly upon us.

The following poem, "The Promising Sun in the Midst of Cloudy Skies" is all about not letting bad circumstances or negative people keep you from seeing the positive side of life. I am amazed at how just a few minutes in the sunshine can really strengthen my spirit after the weather has been cloudy and stormy. After being outside on a beautiful walk one day, I was inspired to write this poem because I was feeling great despair myself, but I knew I had to keep going and wanted to help others along the way.

_____

The Promising Sun in the Midst of Cloudy Skies

I kept wondering when in the world
The rain of misfortune would ever stop.
I felt I was drowning under a wall of water
That made me feel I was about to blow my top.

When I looked up into the sky begging God
To take away these dark, depressing clouds,
I could hear the echo of souls who passed before me
Whisper it will get better somehow.

Not quite sure when my unlucky
Fate would ever change,
All I could see and feel were the cloudy skies
That kept driving me insane.

I walked outside onto a path in the woods
Full of water that was almost over my knees,

Yet no matter how muddy it seemed to get
I felt I had to go through the dirt of life to be set free.

Harsh winds from the dark clouds
Above me blew so hard I could barely walk.
Then the thunder of tough storms roared so loudly
I could not hear myself talk.

Scared and frustrated at the dark clouds
That sent hard rains and winds my way,
I just kept praying to God to give me a sign
That eventually things would get better one day.

After hours of wading in rough waters and
Enduring relentless weather I could not ignore,
I finally saw a light pierce through the clouds
That brightened my gloomy spirit so much more.

Curious to see if maybe that light was the sun
I had missed so much ready to lighten my path,
Somehow the stormy weather around me began
To ease up to help me keep going on the right track.

For quite some time my spirit felt so
Very sad and so heavy for me to control,
Yet when the sun broke through the clouds it healed
The wounds within that tried to damage my soul.

As I came to the end of my path in the woods
The water around me finally disappeared.

I looked at the mountains before me knowing
The sun from God gave me strength to conquer my fears.

After the dreary cloudy skies tried so hard
To block my destiny to achieve a happier life,
The promise of the sun's healing energy was
God's sign that everything would be all right.

CHAPTER 32 - THE RIGHT SIGN AT THE RIGHT TIME

Everything Happens Exactly When It Is Meant to Happen Even When We Do Not Always Understand Why, But We Must Accept God Will Send Signs to Guide Us On the Right Path.

Timing is everything which is a popular saying I have heard all my life, and I really believe that to be so true. When I look back over my past, I remember getting so upset and asking God why this or that had to happen to me. In fact, I just wanted answers and I wanted to know why everything seemed so good for others when I was always the one struggling to make ends meet. I guess you could say I am a poor soul who feels rich in spirit, and I do know that trusting in fate in terms of accepting what happens despite always knowing why is so important.

The following poem, "The Right Sign at the Right Time", is a narrative piece of poetry about one soul who finds herself in Heaven being met by countless angels trying to help her make sense of her often chaotic and troubled life. The further she travels in the afterlife, the more her bad choices and mistakes begin to make sense to her as she learns the right signs really do happen at the right time when we least expect it.

———————————————————

The Right Sign at the Right Time

I was looking within the story of my life
For the right sign at the right time,
But somehow God said there are no clear cut
Answers to solving life's mystic rhymes.

Frustrated and unsure of what
I really was meant to do,
I asked God for a sign to learn to trust that
Sometimes life is often cloudy and blue.

I decided to run away from everything
Just to give my soul a brand new chance.
In my deepest heart I knew I needed
To accept the good and bad of every circumstance.

In my desperate need of a break far
From my life I call an interesting story,
I landed in the midst of Heaven far from home
Where I could now walk the streets of gold in glory.

I came across an angel of faith that told me

I really needed to not give up.
Tears streamed down my face as I cried out,
But I have truly had enough.

As I went a little further an angel of hope
Stopped me right in my tracks.
He said always believe everything happens
For a reason and quit looking so far back.

On the next stop on my journey the angel of love
Embraced my caring heart in a way I so needed to feel.
She just whispered in my ears I will give you
Strength when your soul needs to heal.

When I stumbled down the streets of gold,
The angel of joy caught my eye.
He said you gotta keep smiling even when its hard
And all you want to do is just sit down and cry.

Intrigued by the wisdom I was learning I then
Met the angel of peace who sensed I was in pain.
She just grabbed my hand so I could feel an energy
Of solace melting away all my anxiety and shame.

Determined to find out what
Else my spirit needed to grow,
I ran into the angel of gentleness encouraging Me
I would reap all the good oats I had sowed.

I finally landed at the end of the streets of gold
Greeted by the angel of patience and endurance.

He said I'm sending you back to the world
With a new vision protected by a spirit of great assurance.

Reluctant to leave this Heavenly place for fear
I would find myself trapped in a world of confusion,
Then God whispered to my weary soul
I will give you strength to overcome any false illusion.

So I closed my eyes and took a leap of faith
Back to a new story in my life I hoped to write.
I knew that no matter what happened
God and His angels would help me survive every day and
night.

It is funny how I still look for the right sign at the
Right time even though I never am quite sure.
What I have learned is that life is all about making
The best of it even when there seems to be no cure.

There are still so many times I wonder where
The road signs of life will take my destiny.
Now I know to trust that God has the right sign
At the right time meant for you and me.

CHAPTER 33 - THE ROLLER COASTER RIDE CALLED LIFE

No Matter How Many Ups and Downs Come Our Way, We Have to Trust That Everything Will Work Out for The Best.

I have always known that life is one huge roller coaster ride. Some days it seems everything is going just the way we want it to be. Other times it seems everything is falling apart, and that life is full of one trial right after the next.

I do know that it would be nice if we could always live in the good times, but I know that hard times always come. The key I feel to great change and spiritual growth is to appreciate those times when the waters of life are calm but to understand that when life is not easy we have to keep strong knowing that one day everything will be ok.

The following poem, "The Roller Coaster Ride of Life" is all about the highs and lows we face and learning to value times of peace and to keep fighting with great hope

during times of struggle. There are so many things we cannot control so we must accept the good with the bad and
make the most of every situation God gives us.

The Roller Coaster Ride Called Life

My heart was racing because the
Roller coaster of my life was about to begin.
I prayed to God to keep me strong so
I could learn not to lose and how to win.

As my roller coaster crawled by slowly
To the top of a brand new destiny,
I felt I was living on top of the world
Where nobody could ever get the best of me.

There was a rush of excitement hitting me as the
Roller coaster took me down a hill fast and furious.
I was feeling scared and yet determined to hang onto
This ride even if it made me a little delirious.

When I reached rock bottom I was too nervous
That I would ever make it back to the top.
In the valley of this ride I realized I had been
Hurt so much and my spirit felt sad quite a lot.

Despite my upset I braced myself for a new climb
As my roller coaster took me high in the sky.

Then the track became full of unpredictable
Twists and turns making me feel I was about to die.

Scared to keep going I knew I had come
Way too far to give up anytime too soon.
Then my roller coaster took me into a dark tunnel
Where I felt trapped like a butterfly in a cocoon.

I begged God to let me see the light as it felt
My whole world became too black for me to see.
Somehow I knew I had to go through some dark places
For the sun to guide me to a better path for me.

As I finally reached the end of the dark tunnel
There was stormy weather blocking my view,
Yet even with the rain crashing down I heard God
Whisper don't worry I will always be good to you.

The roller coaster that had become my
Troubled journey seemed it would never end.
I lost control of all the ups and downs and eventually
Hoped my fears would be on the mend.

There were times this roller coaster ride was
Quite fun and full of good times,
Yet I felt jerked around so much I often lost balance
Even when looking for the right signs.

Eventually this roller coaster of a ride I call life
Took me back home where I could stand on my feet.
Now I knew if I could survive this ride

God would give me a second chance to overcome any defeat.

CHAPTER 34 - THE SPIRITUAL MAGIC OF SAFE SEAS

Magical Moments Of Great Healing Can Happen When We Learn to Let Go of Adverse Moments from The Past That Try to Tear Us Apart and Appreciate the Simple Pleasures in Life.

I have always been fascinated with the concept of magic, and I think there are mysteries in this world that certainly cannot be explained. For most people, mystery can happen in different ways and at different times. For me, I have found nature as a way of revealing some of life's most creative discoveries. What I have discovered is that it is better to be open to what nature can teach us. What nature has taught me is to see the beauty in every moment of life. It has also taught me to embrace every single day with great hope knowing that no matter how hard one situation may be, something good will always happen later.

The following poem, "The Spiritual Magic of Safe Seas", is all about listening to the voice of nature. It is all about learning from the mystic air, the refreshing waves of water, and some of nature's finest creatures as they try to teach us all how to let go and relax. I love to be in nature as I feel it helps rejuvenate my often weary soul when I feel overwhelmed. All of my life I have worked hard and sometimes felt I never got truly compensated for all the things I did and the ways I did them. However, any time I allowed myself to spend any time in the great outdoors, I realized that everything would work out because knowing God created such a beautiful universe means that He created a place for me to feel safe and optimistic about the simpler things in life.

The Spiritual Magic of Safe Seas

I was watching the beautiful sky
Fall in love with the great sea.
Then I wondered if somehow there was a message
Of hope lingering in the horizon's mystical destiny.

Somehow I knew that the coastal waters
Where I felt led to explore
Held a secret of great treasures where
I was meant to discover so much more.

I watched seagulls and all kinds
Of birds flying high in the sky.

I knew they had found a freedom that could help
Them stay far from harm away from deceit and lies.

Then in the midst of distress
I listened to the ocean calling my name.
These great seas asked me to make the most
Of my life despite hardship and unending shame.

I could hear waves crashing on the shore as if they
Wanted me to know they did not give up.
These waves washed the shore with such power
Helping me to feel I was good enough.

In the midst of a sunset when night was trying
To bring an end to the sea's journey of a long day,
I could feel a presence of hope embrace my soul
To encourage me to keep the faith and not run away.

I woke up one morning feeling that maybe just maybe
Everything would work out for the best.
The sun pierced through the stormy clouds
To tell me that I needed to find some much needed rest.

I walked the beach picking up seashells
That seemed to stay courageous while broken.
As I carried them in my pocket I felt a peace
Calm my spirit with the most precious words unspoken.

In the middle of the night when the
Whole world was trying to sleep,

I lie awake listening to the safe seas uplift
My sad heart that had often been weary and weak.

It is amazing how a spiritual magic exists in the
Midst of the sea when we all need a place to escape.
Even when reality hits all over again,
I know where I can find true healing so I can feel safe.

There is a spiritual magic that I have come to love
In the miracle of safe seas God has given.
Now I know there is a happiness that lies in
Learning to appreciate the joys of simple living.

CHAPTER 35 - THE SPIRITUALLY CHARMING NECKLACE

Something as Simple as a Keepsake Necklace Can Keep Us Feeling Positive About the Direction Our Lives Are Meant to Travel Even When it Seems the World is Against Us.

When I was much younger, my parents bought me a gold charm necklace with a gold cross coin as a pendant. Every time I wore that necklace, I could feel God was always right by my side. In fact, if I did not have this necklace, then I thought things in my life did not seem right. As I got older, a friend of mine bought me a tree of life pendant that I also took as a sign of good luck. Therefore, I decided to bring my gold cross and tree of life pendants together to create a marriage of perfect balance and harmony.

Then one day, not too long ago, I lost my precious

necklace. To say that I felt alone and lost was certainly an understatement. It was like my good luck charm had been ripped off my neck, and I felt totally isolated from everything that felt truly safe to me. In a state of worry, I looked everywhere for my necklace and often felt I would never find it. Then one day, out of the blue, my gold chain with my precious pendants appeared! I was so happy, and in that moment, I felt I had regained my faith in life again.

The following poem, "The Spiritually Charming Necklace" is all about the story of losing my necklace and finding it again. However, it is an even deeper story about feeling all faith is lost yet discovering with great determination that good things come to those who do not give up.

———————————————————

The Spiritually Charming Necklace

I reached around my neck to
Feel the warmth of your charm.
I needed to feel things would get better if
I just kept the faith you would protect me from harm.

After all the places I have traveled
You never left my side.
When I felt too scared to keep going I could hold my hand
Over you to feel strong so I would not cry.

There were long days of feeling I was just
Too tired to even try anymore.

Yet I could feel the special way you stayed close to my heart
When everyone else walked out the door.

At the end of the day when I would
Lay you down on my treasure chest,
I would just smile at you as your glimmering aura
Encouraged me to get some much needed rest.

Everyday I could wrap you around
My neck just knowing all would be ok.
You had a special way of calming my fears
When the rest of the world just ran away.

Sometimes I could hardly find the right words
To describe how you made me feel.
There was a comforting presence in your cool touch
That was like having a friend that is always real.

It is funny how through the years I often
Took your presence around me for granted.
I just never thought I could lose you because you
Gave me hope and kept me forever enchanted.

Then one day in the midst of all the chaos
Surrounding my often misunderstood life.
I lost you despite my efforts of assuming you would
Always be there and make everything right.

In a state of panic I looked everywhere
Hoping you would never leave me.

Without you there I felt like I was drowning
In a world of my self-created misery.

Days and nights have passed and
Then one day you returned.
Not taking anything too much for granted
Was the lesson I truly learned.

My spiritually charming necklace with the gold cross
And silver tree of life I will always treasure.
I trust these divine signs
Will bring my heart and soul eternal spiritual pleasure.

CHAPTER 36 - THE STRUGGLING KITE IN THE MIDST OF UNPREDICTABLE WINDS

We Often Find Our Greatest Strength in the Midst of Unpredictable Setbacks.

I have always loved walking, and one day when I had a chance to spend alot of time in the great outdoors, I decided to enjoy myself. Not too long after being on my walk, I saw a young child flying a kite. It made me think of how a kite can just float aimlessly in the sky even when the harsh winds are against it.

I remember thinking how great it would be if at some point I could be that kite ready and able to fly anywhere no matter how many odds were trying to break me down.

Even when the winds were rough, I noticed how this kite just kept flying with great courage and strength.

The following poem, "The Struggling Kite in the Midst of Unpredictable Winds", is all about the experience I shared above. It is a poetic reflection of enduring challenging times through the worst of circumstances.

The Struggling Kite in the Midst of Unpredictable Winds

As I was strolling along a path
Trying to understand why,
I found myself barely able to make it
Another step before I began to cry.

Somehow I knew in my heart there
Had to be a sign I could break free.
Then before I knew what to do I saw a child
Flying a bright colorful kite I was meant to see.

The little boy flying this colorful kite
Seemed to be in complete control.
He just gently steered this kite in the direction
He felt the wind wanted it to go.

I could sense this kite was not sure
Which way it should travel,
Yet the gentle wind lifted it high above the trees
Keeping it together so it would not come unraveled.

The winds seemed to pick up speed blowing
This colorful kite in every crazy direction.
But the boy holding it close kept it flying steady
With grace in a moment of sheer protection.

There were moments the winds became weak
And the kite seemed to come spiraling down.
I saw the little boy flash a smile its way
As if to say you got a true friend who will stick around.

Even when it seemed the little boy was tired
Of holding the kite because the winds were uneasy,
The kite just soared right above the clouds
Without fear even when the rest of the world felt queasy.

I was mesmerized in a state of great awe
Thinking I could relate to this kite.
It reminded me of all the times I kept going
Even when things in life did not seem right.

I wished I could be just like this colorful kite
Flying free in solace without any distress.
Even when the winds were strong or weak
This kite found peace in the midst of trials and tests.

My eyes were constantly drawn to this kite
Because I felt God had a message for me to learn.
The way the kite flew in the sky taught me to keep
The faith and I would find answers to my concerns.

I walked away that day thinking of this colorful kite

And the sweet boy who held it close to his soul.
Despite the unpredictable winds they both taught me
It was best to hold on to hope and never let go.

CHAPTER 37 - THE LOVING EYES OF THE ANGEL THAT SAVED MY LIFE

Don't Give Up Because God Sends Angels In Disguise to Comfort Us Most When We Lack the Courage to Free Our Lives from Despair and Heartache.

Sometimes we all need to know someone cares and loves us very much. There are moments when we all feel lost as if nothing matters. There are times when it seems we are so alone hoping someone will take a special interest in us.

I truly believe in angels, and I have felt that God sends them to us during our weakest moments. There have been many times someone crossed my path that I could feel was sent my way to help me through a tough time. I may not have always known this individual was an angel in disguise, but I could feel a spiritual link of great love and mercy just by looking in his eyes.

The following poem, "The Loving Eyes of the Angel that Saved My Life", is all about how one special angel saves the life of one wounded, struggling soul.

———————————————

The Loving Eyes of the Angel that Saved My Life

I fell to the ground with a heart
That had finally grown weary.
It seemed all the familiar things around me
Were no longer peaceful but growing quite eerie.

In a moment of extreme pain
I knew I just wanted to die.
Somehow I could feel the breath of angel's wings
Trying to find the answer every time I asked why.

I could feel the world I left
As if it had never ever existed.
There were moments in the new world I found myself
Where maybe peace would no longer be resisted.

In a world of magical clouds and music
That was harmonious to my ears.
Somehow I discovered in this new world
There would no longer be a reason to drown under my fears.

I walked in amazement hoping that
On this new path I would no longer walk alone.
Then right before my eyes a heavenly presence
Reached for my hand with eyes that pierced my soul.

I could feel something so strong stirring
Within me that I could not fully understand.
All I knew is I wanted to feel a loving heart
Without limits worthy of a second chance.

The angel did not speak to me but it was like
He sent an energy of love that so few people ever get.
I was eager to know his reason for greeting me
And hoping my heart would not suffer another reject.

In a moment of great joy he looked at me
In the most loving, profound ways you could ever see.
I embraced the energy of his eyes with a heart
Longing to find a love to set me free from years of misery.

This angel walked beside me to show me
A new world where everything seemed totally in sync.
It was like no matter where I looked I could see
That this was a time where my heart was finally at peace.

I was greeted by butterflies of all colors that
Seemed to understand I needed a new look on life.
The warmth of the angels hand and his loving eyes
Were a spiritual treasure setting me free from strife.

As my time in Heaven came to an end,

I begged the angel to keep me there.
I realized I did not want to leave
This beautiful place of love and care.

He looked me in the eyes and said
I will always be protecting your soul.
The love I feel for you will be the link connecting
Our spirits and I promise I will never let you go.

CHAPTER 38 - THE WALL OF SPIRITUAL PROTECTION

We Should Know How to Protect Ourselves From Negative Energy By Surrounding Ourselves With A Shield of Great Spiritual Protection.

It was not too long ago that I came to realize I was empathic which basically means that I can feel and sense the energies of others around me. When emotions are high and positive, I feel being empathic is the best blessing ever. However, when the emotions around me are harsh and negative, it can be very difficult trying to protect myself from letting those energies get the better of me.

The following poem, "The Wall of Spiritual Protection", is all about the need to build walls in order to keep ourselves safe from what I call energy vampires. An energy vampire is someone who likes to come around and take the joy away we feel. After being around so many energy vampires in certain scenarios of my life, I was inspired to write the poem below. I realized the only way to survive a negative energy attack is to shield myself from other people and situations that truly do not have my best interests at heart.

The Wall of Spiritual Protection

I decided to build a wall to
Protect me from great harm.
I was sick and tired of pretending to be friendly
With those surrounding me with false charm.

In the middle of all my problems
I knew I had to make a break.
If I continued to give in to the demands of others
I knew I would make a serious mistake.

Every time I turned around there were people
Trying to talk me into things I did not want to do.
I remained in a state of frustration wondering
How I could escape people so superficial and untrue.

Despite the fact that I was so
Agitated beyond complete belief,
I put up a wall of spiritual protection to block
Negative energies drowning me out with their deceit.

This was the kind of wall that I knew
I had to keep up to keep me safe and truly ok.

My enemies would never understand but I could care less
Because I needed to be out of harm's way.

As soon as I built this wall it was amazing
How I finally felt completely protected.
Even when those who pretended to care came close
I could feel their insincere energies were rejected.

I knew I had to keep playing the game just to
Give the appearance that nothing was wrong,
Yet I could hide behind this great wall I built
As if I had escaped into the words of an inspirational song.

Even though those who claimed to be my friends
Never could figure out why I had to be so guarded.
In my deepest thoughts I knew I had to break
The cycle of unending pain that should have never started.

It was amazing how this wall of spiritual protection
Gave me a courage that I never thought I had.
Now I finally felt a new lease on life where I was
Not always feeling so upset and sad.

Each and every moment when the sea of negative energies
Disguised as good tried to bring me down.
Somehow I knew within my heart the wall I built
Would keep them on the outskirts of my serene town.

I finally felt a peace in my spirit that had
Long been unsettled and far from excited.

Now I had a wall of spiritual protection keeping
Me strong and my positive energies fully ignited.

CHAPTER 39 - THE WAVES OF FRESH STARTS AND NEW HOPES

Sometimes The Waves of Life Can Be Rough To Teach Us to Be Strong When Times Are Hard, and Sometimes the Waves Can Be Mild To Teach Us to Appreciates the Calm, Precious Moments When Nature is At Its Best.

I have always been fascinated with ocean waves. Something about the way the water tosses to and fro on a sandy shore is quite fascinating to me. When the waves are rough, it is a true challenge to walk in the water. When the force of waves are so strong it is a challenge for anyone to keep from falling. In many ways I feel life is the same way. When challenges befall us, it is all we can do to stand strong in the middle of trying times.

When the ocean waves are calm and soothing, it feels their gentle greeting around my feet is like receiving a warm embrace from a trusted friend. In many ways when the waves of life are smooth, we can feel at peace knowing that everything is going to work out for the best.

The following poem, "The Waves of Fresh Starts and New Hopes", is all about learning from the waves of life, and trusting that despite the rough times, good times will come again.

The Waves of Fresh Starts and New Hopes

The waves were crashing on the shore of
A new place I wanted to called fresh start
I could hear a voice from Heaven whisper
This is the healing remedy for your wounded heart.

One wave was soft and gentle as if it knew
I needed to heal for real this time.
When it went back into the refuge of the sea
It's like it took away my need to always ask why.

There was another wave that was quite rough
And it almost knocked me off my feat,
Yet I stood strong in my tracks to remind the sea
I had endured much defeat.

Then a new wave came quickly and seemed
To wrap around my legs like a warm, trusted pet.

I could feel a comforting energy in its desire
To help me see the best was to come yet.

In a moment of complete surprise there was
A wave that barely made it my way,
Yet it cried out I know how it feels when your strength
Is low and you barely make it through a day.

As I walked a little deeper into the sea I saw
Another wave wash a sea turtle right past me.
I watched him struggle to survive as if to say
I know what it's like to survive lots of misery.

When the tide was high that day the force of water
Was so strong I had to remain strong not to fall.
Yet in my weary spirit I felt a new destiny awaited me
As I listened to the waves break down my walls.

There were times the waves were a little
Too rough but I knew I had to remain strong.
In the midst of their forceful energies
I knew one day I could make right all my wrongs.

Eventually the tide changed and the waves
Became softer and much easier for me to walk through.
Then I saw a seagull flying above me as if to say
I knew God would keep your spirit strong and true.

As the gentler waves came crashing on the sea
That became a new refuge for my soul,

I thanked God for helping me find the courage
With the help of a few ocean waves not let go.

CHAPTER 40 - TWO BRIDGES AND A NEW PATH

Sometimes We Are Meant to Walk the Path of Pain in Order to Grow Spiritually So That When the Time Comes to Embrace a New Path, We Can Appreciate That True Beauty Rises Out of Chaos.

I love to walk and even more importantly, I love to explore various nature paths. I have found that so many paths offer various things. For instance, there are some paths that seem like the straight and narrow as if they will lead to the best possible place for our hearts to reside. Then there are paths that are full of obstacles making it almost seem impossible for us to overcome.

Throughout my life I have often found myself on paths that I never thought I was meant to travel. It seems the paths upon which I have walked have often been scary and full of so much pain. However, I have also noticed that some paths can be adventurous and lead to a much better way of life. Despite the paths of life, I have discovered I have learned my best lessons when the path was not always clear and when the answers were not always given to me in a way I could understand. It was as if I had to go through the rocky times on my destined path to come out on the other side knowing all would be ok.

In the following poem, "Two Bridges and a New Path", the whole idea is one person's journey of self-discovery. It is the soul's search to find where he or she really belongs and to keep the faith that all things will work out exactly as God has destined them

---

Two Bridges and A New Path

I was walking around
Looking to and fro
When I asked God to give me some
Much needed direction and a place to go.

Then before I knew what was happening
Right before my eyes
I looked up and saw two bridges tempting me
With their persuasive cries.

One of the bridges seemed strong and able
To support me no matter what.
I thought maybe if I walked across this one
It will give me strength to never stop.

Intrigued by the temptation to walk across
This bridge full of new dreams,
I decided to walk the other one first to learn the lesson
That life is not always what it seems.

As I began my journey across this rugged and worn
Out bridge across troubled waters,
I began to feel faint and weary as the
Frustration within me grew hotter and hotter.

I found myself stumbling over all kinds
Of troubled debris in my way,
Yet I was determined to keep going no matter
How bad things got on these crazy days.

In the distance I could see the bridge I should have
Gone down appear to grow so far from me.
I wondered why I thought I had to take
The hard way first and embrace such self-imposed misery.

Somehow I knew that I could
Not quite turn back yet.
The journey across this bridge was hard
But my courage to live my soul would never forget.

As the days and nights passed I often wondered
If I would ever make it to the other side.
Everywhere I turned the winds of pain grew more harsh
And I found myself drowning in constant cries.

I asked God to somehow make the stormy weather stop

So I could reach the end of this path.
He said I know things are hard right now
But you must keep the faith and never look back.

Somehow I knew in my heart that if I just
Remained strong God would see me through.
During the rain I noticed a sweet yellow butterfly
Flying right beside me as if could relate to my blues.

In the middle of my loneliness I felt I needed
A friend to help me get to other side.
I could hear God whisper I love you too much
And sent this butterfly to be your constant guide.

With the strength from God and the presence
Of my new loving, Heavenly friend,
I made it across this bridge to the other side
Determined with a new spirit empowered to win.

As I walked away from this broken bridge
My friend and me decided to find the bridge I gave up.
As soon as we reached the beginning of it,
I knew in my heart that God had now given me new luck.

As I started my new journey across this beautiful bridge
Full of fresh flowers and sunshine in my way,
My friend the butterfly just flew right beside me
With a fresh joy that would never go away.

On this new path God gave us to walk it seemed
That life felt right and completely true.

I learned sometimes you must suffer to grow stronger
So life will be that much better to you.

Every now and then when I am
Reminded of the troubles I have faced,
I just look up to God and thank Him for
Never letting me feel eternally disgraced.

When I think how God sent my new little friend
The butterfly to fly by my side during tough times,
I know God sends miracles to keep us strong
When we need to dance to a new rhythm and rhyme.

CHAPTER 41 - WHAT I CALL THAT LITTLE BUT BIG THING NAMED TRUST

Learning to Trust is Often the Hardest Lesson Of All to Learn When We Have Been Wounded So Many Times, But With Healing and Time, We Can Find the Spiritual Strength to Trust in a Higher Power to Help Us Make Better Judgment Calls When Necessary.

In my past I was always the most trusting soul anyone has ever known. If someone told me something, I honestly believed in his or her word without questions. I guess it was my childhood innocence and the power of blind trust that made me think everyone and everything can be trusted. However, over the course of my adult life, I eventually realized that there are some people and some situations that can't be trusted no matter how much I had wanted otherwise. It has taken alot of heartaches and broken promises for me over the years to realize that trust was something I wished I had learned to understand better.

At this point in my life, I have learned that I can always trust God and the instincts He has given me to assess whether or not a situation is the best for me. Any time I did not trust my instincts I surely paid the price. Now I know if someone or some situation is not being presented in an honest light, I get a feeling to question it further and not invest my heart and soul into something that I know will only cause me trouble.

In the following poem, "What I Call That Little But Big Thing Named Trust", the words are all about what trust is not and all about what it should be. Being honest is something I treasure highly, and in this poem after years of being fooled by the wrong people or misled by a dishonest situation, I learned just how big trust is and never to take it for granted.

What I Call That Little But Thing Named Trust

I was looking around from the top of the sky
To the bottom of the ground
Wondering why I struggled to hear the most sought
After word lost in a world of distressing sounds.

I decided to crawl under the
Biggest shade tree I could find

Hoping to find some release
From my often restless mind.

When I looked within I wanted to know
Why trust was hard for me to embrace.
I was tired of feeling I made a fool of myself again
At the mercy of another disgrace.

Instead of trying to figure it all out
I decided to ask God a thing or two.
I wanted to be able to find a trusted treasure
Of hope in the midst of all my blues.

Frustrated and alone and not sure
If I could trust myself to do the right thing.
God said you are meant to learn from your mistakes
Despite the confusion of a lost dream.

I said God why is it so hard for me to trust
When I know I need to feel safe.
He whispered trust I want to reassure
Your anxious energies with my soothing ways.

I shouted out and asked God why is it every time
I want to trust I find it hard to let down my guard.
He just smiled and said because you have to
Protect yourself from all those false alarms.

Sad and still feeling lost because I felt
I could not reach out like I so wanted,

God said trust me to give you strength
To rise above the negative energies keeping you so haunted.

Unsure if I could take a leap of faith
To open up my heart once again,
God said you have to learn from your pain
To overcome defeat and learn how to win.

I kept shaking my head feeling that all my past hurts
Kept my heart and soul in prison.
God just smiled and whispered trust me
To give you fresh hope and a brighter vision.

Not really knowing how I could get out from under
This tree ready to get the courage to try.
I thanked God for teaching me the importance
Of trust without always asking why.

CHAPTER 42 - WHAT IS THE PURPOSE OF LIFE?

Trying to Find Our Place In This World Is Not Always An Easy Task, But The More We Learn to Be True to Ourselves, The More We Will Feel Good About Who We Are And The Special Soul God Has Designed Us to Be.

Trying to please everyone has been a great weakness for me most of my life. Instead of trying to focus on what I needed to do in order to protect my best interests, I have always been more concerned with how I could help everyone else. I know there is nothing wrong with helping others, but I have learned that it is not always good to do everything all the time just to make sure we make someone else happy.

The key to being true to ourselves is trusting that the purpose of life is to find great happiness within ourselves. After all, if we are not truly happy with who we are, then how can we contribute to the well-being of someone else?

I have encountered many people in my life who seem to be searching for their purpose and the sad thing is that they look for others to help them find out what they are meant to do and who they are meant to be. The purpose of life is all about our own unique self-discovery that we must learn to appreciate every step of the way.

In the following poem, "What is the Purpose of Life", the whole focus is learning to be true to ourselves and learning to enjoy the journey. I really believe life is a great adventure, but sometimes the best part of it is knowing that we do not have to be someone we are not just to make someone else happy. The more we remain at peace with our inner self, the more we will find our purpose is to live and learn and appreciate every minute of this life God has given us.

———————————————

What is the Purpose of Life?

So I took an intriguing survey
To figure out who I really am.
The world thinks they know me
But they truly don't understand.

I was tired of being pulled
Every which way under the sun.
At some point it was my time
To enjoy life and have some fun.

Demands were being made on me
Every way all the time.
I said to heck with conformity
Because I had my own unique rhyme.

Pleasing everyone was so totally
Not for me anymore.
I thought it's time for me to move on
And lose sight of the safe kind of shore.

Something inside of me wanted
To break free and start a new story.
I was tired of going through the motions
Losing sleep due to constant worry.

I thought maybe I would send a prayer
Up to God to help me stay strong.
He said just like the angels around me
You have to find your own happy song.

I searched the music box of my heart
For a tune that could give me peace.
Yet I was not sure if I would ever find
The right song to put my restless heart at ease.

I took a long walk away from all
The chaos trying to hold me back.
I saw birds flying over me as if they were
Angels guiding me on the right track.

I kept getting distracted by thoughts of what

Everyone else wanted me to do.
Yet God kept telling me who cares what others think
Because I will always be good to you.

I kept looking back trying to find why
My past was so full of constant battles and stress,
Yet when I looked forward everything seemed more hopeful
As if my anxiety was put to rest.

Trying to find the purpose of my life was like
Working a great puzzle to make the pieces fit.
I finally accepted what I needed to change
With a spirit determined not to quit.

CHAPTER 43 - WHAT LIES BENEATH

The Mysteries of Our Own Hearts and Souls Teach Us Lessons Of Faith, Hope, and Love If We Listen to Our Inner Voice and Let It Guide Our Choices Rather Than Depending on the Voices of Others.

It is funny because I feel that so much of what we show the world is really not who we are at all. Everyday we play a game of different roles based on the interactions we encounter with family, friends, co-workers, and total strangers. Despite how close or distant a certain interaction may be, I have found that what lies beneath the surface is the true person we really are.

In my younger years, I had no clue who I really was. In fact, I tried to be everything everyone else wanted me to be and lost myself in the process. It took many years of spiritual growth and discovery for me to realize that I am not meant to walk a conventional path and should be proud of who I am. I know I feel so much like a fish out of water no matter where I am, and I honestly feel it is because I am a spiritual soul who will never feel at home until I cross over to the other side.

In the following poem, "What Lies Beneath", the poem focuses on not being afraid to look within to get to know our own selves better. I think the reason I felt lost for so much of my life is because I never took the time to really look within, and when I did, it led to a period of such intense healing energy for me that I knew I needed to get real with myself and try to help others embrace their authentic selves no matter how scary it may be. Being a teacher has also helped me be a healer, and being a healer has enabled me to write words that I hope inspire others to be proud of what lies beneath the surface of the image they project to others.

———————————————————————

What Lies Beneath

What lies beneath the
Delicate surface called me
Is something greater than
I will let the world see.

What lies beneath is something
So beautiful I cant control.
The love I feel is way too strong
For me to ever let go.

What lies beneath is my true self

Dying to break loose.
I am tired of living one way
When connecting to fate is my only truth.

What lies beneath is a link
To a soul a lot like mine.
The rest of the world may be crazy
But I like sharing a love that's kind.

What lies beneath is a dream of what
It would be like to be right by love's side.
I get tired of being trapped under conformity
When my spirit asks why.

What lies beneath is a need to
Not be so scared to take a chance.
I hate not spending time with the truth
Of life despite the circumstance.

What lies beneath is someone
Who needs something more.
My heart feels connected to a trustworthy
Vision that I can't throw out the door.

What lies beneath is a young woman
Realizing her fate needs to change.
As long as my soul stays tied to fear
I will never overcome misfortune's games.

What lies beneath is an intuitive pull
I feel to embrace a different path.

I am tired of pleasing others just to find
Myself always falling off track.

What lies beneath is a heart and soul
Just hoping to stay true to my destiny forever.
Despite life's setbacks I believe
True spiritual love is life's greatest treasure.

CHAPTER 44 -
WHEN THE DARK
NIGHT OF THE SOUL
BECAME A SUNRISE

Even After Experiencing A Dark Night of the Soul, We Can
Trust that The Sun Will Rise Again and a Brand New Start
Awaits Us If We Don't Give Up.

I have always heard that people can go through a dark night of the soul, and for so long I wondered what was meant by that statement. Through many past setbacks, I have truly undergone many dark times, and I finally came to understand that a dark night of the soul is when the negative forces of this life try to drain all the joy and positive energy from your spirit.

I have been undergoing an attack from dark spirits for so much of my life. Because I try to be a positive force in this world, I know that I get often attacked by dark energies wanting me to feel lifeless and suppressed. I could be having the best day in the world, and the minute I walk into a room with negative energy, I have to learn not to let the doom and gloom of someone else cloud my sunny disposition. It has not been an easy task for me, but through every trial and every energy drain, God always brings me out on the other side feeling stronger and more courageous than ever.

In the following poem, "When the Dark Night of the Soul Became a Sunrise", the theme of knowing this too shall pass is evident. I feel that despite how hard life can be, that we can survive and come out stronger on the other side. I have always thought there is such beauty in a sunrise, and when the nights of your life seem like they are too hard to endure, it makes all those sunrises even more admirable and beautiful knowing suffering paves way for a new beginning.

When the Dark Night of the Soul Became a Sunrise

I was tossing and turning
Wishing I could just run away.
Something in the depth of my troubled soul
Would just not let me escape my troubled days.

In the dark of night I could feel
An energy trying to suffocate my soul.

There were voices of despair trying
To choke my spirit so I could not let go.

I got down on my knees wondering
If God could take away my distress.
Somehow I knew I needed spiritual comfort
In the midst of my continual stress.

There were some dark spirits telling me
I would never accomplish my dreams,
Yet something deeper inside me said,
Say a prayer and God will fulfill all your needs.

Confused and scared with a lost soul
That had been torn apart with frustrations over time,
I looked deep in my heart and asked God
To heal my broken spirit for good this time.

I decided to raise my head high to see what
God had in store for me to see.
He said follow the light to the great outdoors
And you will soon discover me.

With an unwilling spirit and a fear
I needed to overcome,
I could feel there was a different spiritual force
Leading me to a new path met by the brilliant sun.

As I opened the door I could see a sunrise
Embracing a mountain top that seemed to catch my eye.

The longer I stared I could feel it wanted me
To listen to a new voice that was free from pride.

I continued to stand in amazement of this sunrise
That seemed to light up the morning.
Somehow in the midst of this light God's spirit
Would protect me and provide much needed warnings.

With a partial smile I could see birds
Of all types flying through the air.
They carried the spirit of freedom and a new life
Where God showed me someone does really care.

I kept staring intently into the ray of colors
The sun cast on the mountain top.
No matter how troubled I had been
God broke through a wall of pain where love once dreamed
a lot.

I asked God to show me what it was
That this sunrise was meant to say.
He just sent a gentle breeze and said
Let it caress your spirit and I promise the pain will go away.

With doubt I was not sure if I could face
A new day with a fresh light of hope to help me feel good,
Yet the sun kept shining its light on the mountains
Like a true friend protecting you the way he should.

I placed my hands together and took a deep breath
To breathe new life into my heart.

Through the grace of God's healing light and a nice sunrise
I knew I was headed for a fresh, new start.

CHAPTER 45 - WHY FIGHT SAID THE ANGEL?

Sometimes We Must Stay Strong No Matter How Much We Want To Give Up Because We Have to Accept that Bad Things Do Happen to Good People And That is Ok.

Struggle and frustration seem to be the common road-blocks so many of us face today. In a world drowning under harsh circumstances, it is so hard to stay positive. In my own life, keeping my head above water when I felt the ocean currents of life were dragging me under has been a constant battle. I have had so many crazy things to happen and wondered like so many of us, why me?

What I have come to learn is I am not meant to know why, and I must trust that God has the right answers all the time. One day I thought about what if angels get tired of doing good deeds sometimes and want to just quit being the good Samaritans they are. Then I realized that, despite how tired they must get, the angels of this life never give

195

up. They persevere through all the storms of life and come out stronger on the other side because they believe that good things come to those who wait.

In the following poem, "Why Fight Said the Angel?", the theme of angels fighting and not giving up is evident throughout the entire poem. This poem is a reflection of how spiritual energy is strong enough to overcome every problem as long as we do not lose heart or our faith that eventually the problems we are facing will be overcome in time.

Why Fight Said the Angel

At the end of the day
I wondered what it was all for.
Maybe if I ended it all everyone else
Would realize I was not worth that much more.

I tried and tried to figure out
How I could begin again,
Yet some darkness inside me kept
Bringing me down so I would lose instead of win.

There were times I was not sure
Which way I should go.
It seemed I would rather give up than walk
Around pretending there was more I needed to know.

I was frustrated and hoping
My fate would somehow change,
Yet every time I wanted to keep going
I could not conquer my turmoil and pain.

Everyone thought I was so happy but
They really do not know me at all.
Sometimes I feel I am headed for
The greatest and most destructive fall.

I tried to figure out what
In the world I should do,
Yet I could never feel good about myself
Because I was tired of feeling blue.

I got down on my knees hoping
Somehow my life would get better,
Yet I could not figure out how to endure
All the hard times and survive the stormy weather.

I thought maybe I could just run away
And try to leave everything I had known.
Then a voice within cried out your heart
Is too far from the place it calls home.

In times of uncertainty when I felt
I really needed to take a break,
I kept drowning in sadness
Because of all my tragic mistakes.

Unfortunately there were no answers

For why my life was so crazy.
All I could see were gray clouds
When the sky was blue and far from hazy.

There are times I wonder if I will ever be able
To stand strong in the midst of distress.
Now I know that no matter how hard life is
I have to put my weary soul to rest.

CHAPTER 46 - WRAPPED UP IN A DAYDREAM

Sometimes It is Good to Escape Into a Good Daydream As It Gives Us A Chance to Embrace A Life That Makes Us Feel Happy and Strong.

I truly love to daydream. Ever since I was a child, I have loved being able to embrace nice fantasies. Now that I am older, I honestly love it even more. Because life can be so ordinary and routine at times, it is nice to escape the everyday mundane tasks of this world into one that is much more fulfilling.

I think daydreaming is something everyone should do because being able to imagine being in a different place at a different time is quite powerful. When I really use my imagination, I can embrace a world where I truly want to be, and I can spend time with the people I love there without worries or demands on my time.

The following poem, "Wrapped Up in A Daydream",
is all about taking a journey into a different place and time
to another world where life is much more enjoyable and
fun to experience. It is a reflection of a universal cry for
help to be heard and carried away into a beautiful fantasy
where life is always happy and peaceful.

Wrapped Up in a Daydream

I was wrapped up in daydream
To take me far away from here.
No matter what came my way I was determined
To let the power of courage conquer my fear.

This was my time to take a trip into
A much more spiritual way of life.
I was sick and tired of living a half-hearted existence
And knew I needed to get things right.

In the everyday go with the flow I could make
Anyone see I was doing just fine,
Yet within my weary spirit I knew I was eager
To break free from it all this time.

Somehow I could feel a new destiny calling my name
To take a walk on a new path of hope.
After all my upsetting circumstances
I knew a better dream awaited me where I could finally cope

From the top to the bottom of a life
That seemed to confine my spirit to and fro,
I was sick and tired of living for everyone else
And was ready to really let go.

After years of pretending to be someone
I never really was at all.
I had finally learned that not being
True to myself was my greatest fault

In the heart of my mind I could see
Images of a world where peace always existed.
It was like the negative energy of situations
Could not affect me because this time my soul resisted.

In the daydream I created I learned
There was so much good joy to spread around.
The frustrating energies of life could not withstand
The more comforting place my heart had found.

I realized I could create my own fate
With the strength from God to never hold back.
Even though my previous life was full of disappointment
My daydream got me back on track.

Within my special dream it felt as if
My new life finally made some real sense.
I could live an authentic journey now
Without all the hype and careless suspense.

It's funny because the outside world

Keeps looking for me hoping I will some day return,
Yet in my lovely daydream enjoying the
True beauty of life had finally become my turn.

CHAPTER 47 - UNFINISHED BUSINESS BETWEEN GOD AND ME

Sometimes We Try to Make a Deal With God to Make Life Better For Us When We Often Are Meant to Go Through Hard Times to Grow Stronger Spiritually So We Can Face Anything.

I have often heard people talk about how they like to make deals with God. Somehow if they can get God to do what they want, then everything will fall into place for them. I also know that no matter how much we bargain with God, there are so many things in this life that are meant to happen for a reason.

I am not like most people, and I feel that I think or do things so differently than many others because I like to focus on the spiritual aspect of this world. Anytime I questioned God about something because I did not understand, He always gave me the courage to just know everything would work out for the best. I often had to go though hell on earth to get there, but eventually He helped me find my way to a better avenue of life.

In the following poem, "Unfinished Business Between God and Me", the story is shown of one person's trip to Heaven to make a deal with God. However, what the person in the poem discovers is that God wants him to learn that life is not meant to be easy, and the hard times only make us stronger and able to overcome anything.

Unfinished Business Between God and Me

I fell deep asleep into a dream searching
For God hoping to make a good deal.
So I left everything I had ever known
In search of a life that was truly real.

During the midst of the greatest aggravations
I had ever seen and heard,
I stood right in the middle of the chaos of my life
Thinking one day there would be no more hurt.

My mind kept pulling me back to
A time when life was always good,
Yet I always felt empty even
When I did the best I could.

My heart tried to get me to understand

All the pain that surrounded my life,
Yet when I tried to find some peace
All I heard were the cries of unending strife.

Frustrated with my life and ready to make
A brand new deal for a change.
I finally made it to Heaven hoping
God would bring an end to my constant pain.

I looked into God's bright face saying
I promise I will be all your ever wanted.
He whispered I know you are pulled in
Many directions keeping your spirit forever haunted.

I then asked God why is it life
Always seems so completely unfair.
He just said because sometimes you have
To be hurt to find out there are those who do care.

In a spirit of true curiosity I asked God
Why I always felt like I was hitting the biggest wall.
He smiled and said because I want you
To forgive yourself for all the things that were never your fault.

With tears in my eyes I asked God
Why I never could feel happy for so long.
He said listen closely to the words of hope
When you listen to the next love song.

Confused because I felt God had allowed

Too many setbacks to throw me off track.
He said I know what you are always thinking
And I let you fall so you can learn not to look back.

Eager to understand why God let others always
Have the good life while I seem so sad and blue,
He just kindly sent a gentle breeze to let me know
To keep the faith even when I felt like a fool.

Wondering when I would ever find a way
Out of a life I so no longer could take.
God said just hold on to hope and trust
That things will get better one day.

As I searched the sky I cried out to God
And asked Him why many times he remained so silent.
He said remember the rainbows I sent to calm you
When the storms in your life were violent.

After all the talk I had with God that day
I really kept struggling to find the answers to all things.
God said I know what you are thinking
And you got to be strong when you feel you are going
insane.

I woke up from my dream amazed at how God and
I took care of some unfinished business that night.
Even though I still had to face my problems,
I finally realized everything would be all right.

CHAPTER 48 - WHEN DISAPPOINTMENT TOOK MY SOUL ON A TRIP

There Will Be Times In Life When it Seems the Whole World is Against Us, But We Must Not Lose Heart and Trust that Every Setback We Experience Happens to Teach Us To Hang In There.

Disappointment is truly a word my heart and soul knows so well. I have had so many people and situations throughout my life to let me down. I know what it is like to put all your hope and trust into something only to have those dreams not to come true. I also know what it is like to think you can really trust someone only to have that person let you down.

In the following poem, "When Disappointment Took My Soul on A Trip", I tell the story of my own life and how through various experiences I learned not to let what brought me down keep me down forever. It is often very hard to keep our heads above water when life is difficult, and it is human nature to strive for the best and to want to overcome harsh circumstances. Just remember that when disappointment takes your soul on a trip there is always a reason why certain things did not go the ways we thought they should go.

========

When Disappointment Took My Soul on A Trip

Once upon a time there was
A force so strong it choked my soul.
His name was disappointment,
And he said I will never let you go.

I did not understand why this dark force
Of nature wanted to isolate me so much.
He said I will take you on a trip into the real world
Where all your hopes and dreams are too hard to touch.

Lost and confused I refused to take such a trip
With something that cared less about me.
He just said you gotta hold on tight because
I will show you all the moments others left you in misery.

As the trip began I was shown so called friends
From my past that I thought I could trust,
And then disappointment said these people

Were more concerned about themselves than your good
luck.

I begged disappointment to stop
Dragging my soul into my painful past.
He just looked me dead in the eye and said
You gotta face your fears because they are here to last.

Upset and frustrated I did not want
To continue this difficult trip.
Disappointment just laughed in my face and said
There will always be people who are going to make you sick.

I was desperate to escape this forced journey
Disappointment wanted me to face,
Yet I was forced to take a long hard look
At all the times I felt like such a disgrace.

I could see a time as a child I just wanted
Someone to love me with a kind word,
But all disappointment did was let me see
The times other kids left me lost in lonely world.

As the journey got longer disappointment showed me
Times as a teenager when I felt left out of the cool kids
games.
I can remember feeling those times I felt ridiculed
And left alone feeling sad and so ashamed.

When he took me into my twenties I could see
All the so called friends who let me down.

All they really cared about was using me
To turn my smile into an everlasting frown.

So depressed I just asked disappointment
When this weary travel would stop.
He just said you gotta face this next decade
Before you find a way to get your stomach out of knots.

With tears in my eyes I was not sure
How much more I could take.
When I was taken into my thirties I was shown
Caring too much was my greatest mistake.

I asked disappointment why I had to be
Reminded of all the times he never walked away.
He just said because you had to face the hurt
To find the strength to escape your present tragic fate.

I looked within and tried to find if there was
Any faith left inside from which I could use.
Because I knew that somewhere God was always there
Helping me find a way out of my broken promises and mis-
guided issues.

As I woke the next morning I could still feel
All the pain disappointment brought me in a dream.
Even in a magical escape of a night's rest the reality
Is life is never as easy as it may seem.

I got out of bed and decided to say a prayer
To see if God could help me face another hard day.

Even in the midst of my lingering distress
God helped me face disappointment with much greater
faith.

CHAPTER 49 -
WHEN I DECIDED
TO LEAVE IT ALL
BEHIND

Sometimes Taking A Good Break From All the Pressures Of Life Is Exactly What We Need to Restore Our Weary Souls and Become Strong Enough to Face Anything that Comes Our Way.

We all face pressures in life. It would be nice if life was just one huge rose garden, but honestly to expect a life with no upsets would just not make sense. There will always be times that seem overwhelming, and I have found that when life gets to be a little too hard to handle, that having an escape route is often a really good thing. I know that we cannot run away from our problems because eventually we have to face things no matter how hard they may be. However, what I have discovered is that facing our problems is so much easier if we can take some time out to gain a fresh new perspective on life.

In the following poem,"When I Decided to Leave it All Behind", I wrote this piece of poetry as a reflection of my frequent desire to hide out from the world. Being an empathic soul has often been a blessing and a curse for me throughout my entire life. When I am picking up the negative feelings of other people's energy on top of my own personal stresses, I almost become so mentally and physically tired I can barely function. After going through so many times like this, I decided to write a poem reflecting on the need we all have to just get away from everything.

When I Decided to Leave It All Behind

I was looking out the window watching
The rain come crashing down.
Within my weary soul I wondered
If anyone would miss me if I left town.

Inside of me was a strong desire to escape
All the pressure I had been under.
I could feel my spirit struggling as if all the joy within
Had been drowned out by cruel thunder.

Unsure if running away was the
Answer to all of my distress,
I kept trying to tell myself to keep the faith
But I could not find any peaceful rest.

It was not too long something inside

Of me began to come apart.
I was sick and tired of continual setbacks
Always hurting my injured heart.

I thought of the pros and cons of sticking
Around and was not sure what to do,
Yet I just wanted to find some true hope
Without always feeling like a fool.

Everywhere I turned I was feeling pulled
In so many puzzling directions.
I tried to figure out how to be strong to
Withstand the world's constant rejection.

Some days I felt like everything in my
Life was truly going to be ok,
Yet as soon as I started to feel better some
Deceptive spirit always tried to lead me astray.

My heart was telling me that I needed a
Brand new change to get my life together.
Negative energy was trying to convince me
I had to stay unhappy even if it was sunny weather.

Confused and hoping God would help me
Find the right path for my life,
I prayed with all my heart and soul that
Somehow everything would turn out all right.

It seemed every day of my existence
Became a constant struggle to endure,

Yet the voice of God within always whispered
Hold my hand when you feel so unsure.

Despite the voice of logic trying to tell me
I had to please everyone despite my own frustration,
God said sometimes you have to let go of
What's not working to finally escape your desperation.

CHAPTER 50 - WHY OH WHY?

It Is Human Nature to Question Why Certain Things Happen, But Often We Must Accept That Some Things Are Not Meant For Us To Understand No Matter How Much We Want To Know the Reasons.

Asking why to figure out why so many bad things happen to good people is a universal question to problems we may never find a way to resolve. I have found myself questioning so many of the events from my past and wanting so much to understand why I had to get hurt so much. Even now I often question God and try to figure out why certain issues are taking place in my life.

In the following poem, "Why Oh Why", the whole idea of asking this question is presented in so many different scenarios. The truth is some answers we receive may not be what we were hoping for, but the questions we ponder often lead to changes that are meant to make our lives stronger and to put us on the right track to greater happiness.

Why Oh Why?

Why oh why is it the harder I try
The more I feel I will fail?
Then I just face a new day praying for
A newfound strength to prevail.

Why oh why is it I just feel I can barely
Make it through another long day?
Then somehow God sends a free spirited bird along
To remind me to keep the faith all the way.

Why oh why is it that I cannot seem to escape
The struggles that seem to engulf my very soul?
Yet when I feel like giving up I bask in nature's sun
With a radiance from Heaven that caresses me so.

Why oh why is it that when I care so much
And try so hard to make things right?
Someone tries to bring me down again
With their false pretenses and misguided lies.

Why oh why is that some people's lives
Always seem to fall into the right place?
But then I find myself feeling like a fool
Because I became a victim again to deceptive ways.

Why oh why is it that I have searched the world over
To figure out why I seem to get hurt more than I should?

God then sends a rainbow after a storm to
Remind me sometimes we often feel misunderstood.

Why oh why is it that my heart seems like it is
Being torn apart in so many pieces I cannot fix?
Yet when I hold my hand over my chest I feel
A love warm my soul to keep me from falling so sick.

Why oh why is it that I can still go the extra mile
To help another and still feel so incomplete?
Then I see a broken-winged butterfly struggling
To fly because its drowning in defeat.

Why oh why is it that I can't seem to escape
All the energies that try to drain me dry?
Can the energy vampires get the point
They are the reason I keep asking so many whys.

Why oh why is it that I fight so hard to
Make sure others really know how I feel?
When I feel my efforts are hopeful I feel a peace
Within calm my restless spirit keeping it still.

Why oh why do I feel like I am running
In circles about to lose my mind?
Then I have a good cry and know that
God is the anchor to my soul through all my bad times.

Why oh why do I keep searching for answers
To questions that I feel will never quit?

.

When life looks hopeless I can look above
And pray God heals the wounds within I need fixed.

Why oh why is life so hard
For any of us to endure?
Maybe we are meant to struggle
Before we find a love so pure.

Why oh why is life a never ending ocean of
Unanswered questions to our search for direction?
I know no matter how lost I may feel,
God will comfort my soul with His everlasting protection.

AFTERWORD

Now that we have reached the end of our courageous journeys, I hope you feel even more positive and encouraged than ever. I hope that every message and every poem made you realize that you are not alone in your pain, and that one day everything will make sense. Even if your life seems very confusing and unhappy right now, just remember that courage is the true spiritual force God gives us all to help us rise above the afflictions that bring us down. With courage, you can heal from the past and find strength to face anything that comes your way.

I have spent so much of my life lacking courage. It has been a long journey for me to get to the place where I know that no matter what happens everything will be ok. Everything I have shared with you in this book has come from a very personal place and experience for me. However, the lessons I learned and the creative insight I was given have helped me heal and made me realize that writing this book was true divine intervention.

ABOUT THE AUTHOR

After writing my first book, *Spiritual Whispers to the Soul*, which I self-published in July of 2012, I decided I wanted to continue my path of creative and inspirational writing. Presently I am a full-time computer technology instructor for a community college in Boone, NC. Even though I am thankful for my job, I am even more thankful to be able to keep pursuing my passion for writing. For me writing my first book and my current one, *Living and Learning From the Healing Waters of Courage*, has been such a great adventure for me because I love to help heal and inspire others as they search for meaning in their lives.

My goal is to continue to self-publish more books under my publishing name, Colorful Spirit Publishing, in the hopes I can be what motivates others to follow their true spiritual paths in life. For more information on where to find my first book and my current one for sale, please visit my website at www.colorfulspirit.com or feel free to email me at hwright@colorfulspirit.com. I hope that somehow my first book as well as this one can continue to be a great source of inspirational comfort to the lives of so many now and forever.

www.ingramcontent.com/pod-product-compliance
Lightning Source LLC
Chambersburg PA
CBHW031544040426
42452CB00006B/181